1952–2012

DIAMOND JUBILEE SOUVENIR MAGAZINE

ELIZABETH
THE QUEEN

COVER AND PHOTO: © PRESS ASSOCIATION IMAGES/JOHN WARBURTON-LEE PHOTOGRAPHY/ALAMY/ANDY MYATT

Above: Queen Elizabeth II, photographed in 1950 before her accession

A WARM WELCOME TO OUR Diamond Jubilee souvenir magazine, which celebrates The Queen's remarkable 60-year reign. Her Majesty Queen Elizabeth II is only the second British monarch to achieve this anniversary; it is a significant and historic moment for Britain. Over the following pages, we chart The Queen's life: her idyllic childhood and happy marriage to Prince Philip – Duke of Edinburgh, the birth of her four children and eight grandchildren, and the many official engagements, interesting occasions and iconic moments. We hope you enjoy this special publication in celebration of Britain's Diamond Jubilee year.

Sam Pears, Editor

ELIZABETH – THE QUEEN

Published by The Chelsea Magazine Company Ltd, Liscartan House, 127-131 Sloane Street, London SW1X 9AS. Tel: +44 (0)20 7901 8000. Fax: +44 (0)20 7901 8001.
Editor Sam Pears **Deputy Editor** Jessica Tooze **Art Editor** Gareth Jones **Contributors** Camilla Tominey and Chris Fautley
Advertisement Manager Julian Strutt **Sales Executive** Alex Lobsang **Commercial Director** Vicki Gavin **Deputy Managing Director** Steve Ross **Managing Director** Paul Dobson
Printed in England by Wyndeham Heron, Maldon, Essex **Production** All Points Media

Distribution USA and Canada: CMG, LLC/155 Village Blvd/3rd Floor/Princeton, NJ 08540 USA. Rest of World: COMAG, Tavistock Road, West Drayton UB7 7QE. Tel: +44 (0)1895 444055. Fax: +44 (0)1858 445255

ETTINGER
LONDON

QUINTESSENTIAL BRITISH
LEATHER GOODS SINCE 1934

www.ettinger.co.uk

PHOTO: PRESS ASSOCIATION IMAGES

Contents

A special thank you to **The Duke of Marlborough** for his contribution to this publication. Thanks also to our contributors **Camilla Tominey**, Royal Editor of the *Sunday Express* in London and royal expert for the USA television network NBC, and to **Chris Fautley**, London expert and regular contributor to BRITAIN magazine.

From the Duke of Marlborough

The 11th Duke of Marlborough, John Vanderbilt Spencer-Churchill, writes from his home – Blenheim Palace, Oxfordshire

IT IS A VERY SPECIAL YEAR IN BRITAIN, as 2012 marks Her Majesty Queen Elizabeth II's Diamond Jubilee. It is an historic moment. Having ascended to the throne in 1952 at the tender age of 25, The Queen follows in the footsteps of her great-great-grandmother Queen Victoria, who reigned from 1837 to 1901 and who was the last and only other monarch to reach this major anniversary. Including Queen Victoria, only five other kings and queens in British history have reigned for 50 years or more.

In the six decades since HM The Queen's succession, Britain has seen huge social, political and economic change; The Queen has remained a constant and stable figure at the head of the world's most famous Royal Family. During her reign, The Queen has given regular audience to no fewer than 12 Prime Ministers, from Winston Churchill (who was, of course, born here at Blenheim Palace, and is buried in nearby Bladon) to our present Prime Minister David Cameron.

The Queen's role as monarch extends to much more than audiences with Prime Ministers; the vows made ▶

Above: The Duke and Duchess of Marlborough in the grounds of Blenheim Palace. *Right:* The Gold State Coach bearing The Queen and The Duke of Edinburgh on the way to Buckingham Palace following the Coronation. *Next page:* The Queen and The Duke of Edinburgh with their immediate family; The Queen and British Prime Minister David Cameron

on Coronation Day were for life; the role is demanding and never ending – The Queen is always "at work".

Her Majesty has attended every opening of Parliament except those in 1959 and 1963, when she was expecting Prince Andrew and Prince Edward respectively. The Queen is currently patron of over 600 charities and organisations, over 400 of which she has held since 1952. She has personally held over 610 investitures, has sent almost 540,000 telegrams to couples in the UK and the Commonwealth who are celebrating their diamond wedding (60 years) anniversary, and has given out approximately 90,000 Christmas puddings to staff, continuing the custom of King George V and King George VI.

In 60 years, The Queen has undertaken 261 official overseas visits, including 78 State Visits to 116 different countries, and has attended 56 Royal Maundy services in 43 cathedrals. During her reign, a total of 6,710 people have received Maundy Money in recognition of their service to the Church and their communities. The Queen also supports service to others, through close relationships with the voluntary and charitable sectors. About 3,000 organisations list a member of the Royal Family as patron or president.

Formal duties are balanced with family values as The Queen highlighted in her 2011 Christmas speech.

The Queen spoke about unity and hope in the face of adversity and the importance of family during the year that two of her grandchildren were married. The Queen and The Duke of Edinburgh also celebrated their 64th wedding anniversary that year, on November 20, 2011. They have four children, eight grandchildren and one great-grandchild. Family life has been an essential support to The Queen throughout her reign and, like many of us, the family always spend Christmas together (at Sandringham in Norfolk).

We shall be celebrating the Queen's Diamond Jubilee here at Blenheim Palace with a succession of special entertainment over the Bank Holiday weekend, including appearances by classic British children's characters, The Bunbury's Celebrity Cricket Match followed by afternoon tea on the South Lawn, and a Massed Brass Band Concert. You will receive a warm welcome should you choose to celebrate the festivities with us. But, wherever you are, I hope you enjoy this special Diamond Jubilee publication, which commemorates The Queen's exceptional life and leadership. Long May She Reign.

Marlborough.

The 11th Duke of Marlborough

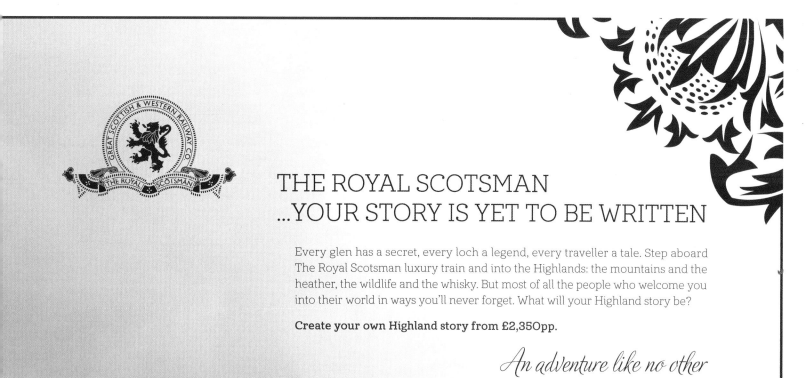

THE ROYAL SCOTSMAN
...YOUR STORY IS YET TO BE WRITTEN

Every glen has a secret, every loch a legend, every traveller a tale. Step aboard The Royal Scotsman luxury train and into the Highlands: the mountains and the heather, the wildlife and the whisky. But most of all the people who welcome you into their world in ways you'll never forget. What will your Highland story be?

Create your own Highland story from £2,350pp.

An adventure like no other

LL 0845 164 5441, +44 (0)20 3117 1588 OR CONTACT YOUR LOCAL TRAVEL AGENT. ORIENT-EXPRESS.COM

1926–1952

From Princess to Queen

The first child of The Duke and Duchess of York, Elizabeth stood third
in the line of succession to the throne. It was not expected that her father would become
King, or that the beautiful young Princess would become Queen

Previous page: **1926** The Queen Mother with her husband (then The Duke and Duchess of York) and their daughter at her christening; **1949** Looking beautiful, Princess Elizabeth wears a silver gown with a diamond tiara and pearl necklace. *Above:* **1937** The young Princess perfects her wave. *Below:* **1939** Princesses Elizabeth and Margaret's first ride on a Tube train, a novel experience mingling with "ordinary" passengers. *Right:* **1944** Five days before Princess Elizabeth turned 18 at Sandringham, the King's country home in Norfolk. Wartime conditions curtailed celebrations, yet she received congratulations from all over the British Commonwealth

Princess Elizabeth Alexandra Mary, or "Lilibet" as she was known to her family, enjoyed an idyllic childhood. Described as the "happiest family in the world", The Duke of York thought of his family as one, not four people. Schooled at home, Elizabeth and her younger sister Princess Margaret would spend their spare time riding horses, playing with their pet corgis and putting on pantomimes for family and friends. But the Yorks' cosseted world was shattered in 1936, when within a year of succeeding his father George V as King, Edward VIII abdicated to marry American divorcee Wallis Simpson. His shy younger brother "Bertie", who had struggled with a stammer all his life, suddenly found himself on the throne on the brink of the outbreak of World War Two.

The war years proved to be the making of George VI, who with the his wife made morale boosting visits throughout the UK, visiting bomb sites and munitions factories. The young Elizabeth played her part too, joining the Women's Auxiliary Territorial Service, where she trained as a gunner and mechanic.

By then she had fallen in love with a handsome young Naval officer with whom she had been exchanging letters since 1939.

Her wedding to Prince Philip on November 20, 1947, could not have come at a better time for Britain, still reeling from the horrors of war. Almost exactly a year later, Prince Charles was born, with Princess Anne arriving in 1950.

With her father's health deteriorating, Elizabeth had been frequently standing in for him at public events and in 1952 it was announced that she and Philip would tour Australia and New Zealand via Africa, on his behalf. The couple were in Kenya on February 6, 1952 when word arrived of the death of George VI. Having left as a princess, Elizabeth returned to Britain the following day as Queen.

Right: **1947** The newlyweds. Princess Elizabeth leaves Westminster Abbey in London, with her new husband, The Duke of Edinburgh, on November 20, 1947 after their wedding ceremony. The Queen's beautiful wedding dress was designed by Sir Norman Hartnell

Above: **1945** A time for celebration, as Britain's Prime Minister Winston Churchill, centre, joins the Royal Family, from left, Princess Elizabeth, Queen Elizabeth, King George VI, and Princess Margaret, on the balcony of Buckingham Palace in London, on VE-Day on May 8, 1945. *Below:* **1939** How times have changed – unrecognised by passers-by, Princess Elizabeth, left, and her sister Princess Margaret, are taken for a walk through busy London streets on May 15 following their first ride on a London Underground train

Above: **1950** Princess Anne is born on 15 August. Here she takes centre stage at Buckingham Palace on 21 October, the day of her christening. Also present are Vice Admiral the Earl Mountbatten of Burma, Princess Margarita of Hohenlohe-Langenburg, Hon Andrew Elphinstone, Princess Alice Countess of Athlone, and a young Prince Charles with his back to camera

THE ONLY JAGUAR TO OFFER ROOM SERVICE

Introducing The Jaguar Suite at 51 Buckingham Gate

5¹ BUCKINGHAM GATE
Taj Suites and Residences

For more details and bookings please call 020 7769 7766
or email reservations@51-buckinghamgate.co.uk

TAJ
Hotels Resorts
and Palaces

51 BUCKINGHAM GATE | LONDON SW1E 6AF | UNITED KINGDOM | 020 7769 7766

Above left: **1936** Ten-year-old Elizabeth in New York with her uncle, The Prince of Wales, before he became King. While much of America might have been stirred by the chance of Mrs Simpson becoming a queen, England thought otherwise and Edward's abdication in order to marry his love propelled Elizabeth into the role of Crown Princess. *Above right:* **1938** Princess Elizabeth and her companion Shaun Plunket, take the penguins for a walk at London Zoo. *Below left:* **1948** Princess Elizabeth admires her infant son, Prince Charles Philip Arthur George, at Buckingham Palace. *Below right:* **1945** Princess Elizabeth undergoing training at an ATS Training Centre in southern England

Above: **1941** The sisters go together like a horse and carriage – here, confident looking, Princess Elizabeth and Princess Margaret are in the garden of their wartime country residence (Windsor), where they are staying during the Second World War. In view of the need for saving petrol, their Royal Highnesses' ponycart has again been brought in to use

Above: **1938** The King and Queen, and Princesses Elizabeth and Margaret Rose, being welcomed on their arrival at Olympia, London. *Above right:* **1942** Princess Elizabeth (right) discusses a point or two concerning a pantomine with her mother, while her sister Princess Margaret Rose looks on demurely. The two princesses took the leading roles in "Cinderella". *Right:* **1936** HM The Queen's love of dogs began early. Here the young Princess Elizabeth has a Pembrokeshire Corgi in her arms as the cameraman catches the two children of The Duke and Duchess of York in a fun-loving mood.
Below: **1935** Princess Elizabeth waving to the crowd, with her grandfather George V and HM Queen Mary on the balcony of Buckingham Palace after attending the Jubilee service at St Paul's Cathedral

For a limited time,

SAVE $10*

When you book a First Class BritRail London Plus Pass, BritRail England Pass or BritRail Pass.

With our special Diamond Jubilee coupon code, available at www.britrail.com/diamondjubilee

Join in the celebrations of

THE QUEEN'S DIAMOND JUBILEE by planning YOUR VERY OWN VISIT to Britain this summer!

Discover Britain's Royal Heritage and so much more by exploring England, Scotland and Wales with a BritRail Pass.

When traveling with a BritRail Pass, enjoy the freedom to travel as often as you want, when you want, hopping on and off trains at your leisure.

And even get a taste of the royal treatment with BritRail's First Class Passes!

Exclusively by

Above: **1944** A family photograph taken on Princess Elizabeth's 18th birthday. *Left:* **1947** The happy couple, Princess Elizabeth and Lieutenant Philip Mountbatten, were at Clydebank to attend the launch of the liner RMS Caronia, but stopped by at the town hall en route to receive the town's wedding present – an electric sewing machine. *Below:* **1933** There was always time for child's play – Princess Elizabeth rides a tricycle in the park

Above: **1949** Proud parents, Princess Elizabeth and The Duke of Edinburgh hold their first child Prince Charles, aged six months. *Right:* **1952** Dressed in black Queen Elizabeth II sets foot on British soil for the first time since her accession, as she lands at London Airport after her day and night flight from Kenya following the death of her father, King George VI. Having left as a princess, Elizabeth returned to Britain the following day as Queen. *Left:* **1952** The coffin containing the body of King George VI is carried towards the Royal Train. Veiled in black The Queen, The Queen Mother, Princess Margaret, and The Princess Royal can be seen

1952–1962

The Crowning Glory

More than a year after her accession the Crown Princess was welcomed in as HM Queen Elizabeth II. Large crowds of people turned out to view the procession, despite very heavy rain. It would prove to be a busy decade for Her Majesty

The Coronation of Queen Elizabeth II on June 2, 1953 marked an exciting new era for the House of Windsor. The ceremony in Westminster Abbey was televised for the very first time. Twenty million British viewers gathered around black-and-white television sets. A four-year-old Prince Charles was pictured looking bored by all the pomp and pageantry although he and his two-year-old sister delighted in watching the crowds from the Buckingham Palace balcony.

The Queen, ever conscious of her duty to the Commonwealth, set about meeting her subjects and launched the Royal Yacht *Britannia*. She and Prince Philip embarked on a six-month around-the-world tour; Her Majesty was the first reigning monarch of Australia and New Zealand to visit those nations. During the trip, three quarters of the population of Australia were thought to have seen The Queen.

In 1957, she made a State Visit to America, where – as well as addressing the United Nations General Assembly – she stayed at the White House with the Kennedys. She travelled on to Canada, where she became the first monarch to open a parliamentary session.

With such a busy schedule, family life had to take a back seat to duty. It was not until 1960 that The Queen gave birth to her third child, Prince Andrew, said to be the baby she had "for herself". A year later she was back on tour, visiting Cyprus, India, Pakistan, Nepal and Iran before travelling to Ghana and Sierra Leone. The then Prime Minster Harold Macmillan would later write of the hard-working monarch: "She has indeed the heart and stomach of a man. She loves her duty and means to be a Queen."

Above: **1953** Queen Elizabeth II gives a wide smile for the crowd from her carriage as she leaves Westminster Abbey, London after her Coronation. *Right:* **1953** The Gold State Coach, bearing The Queen and The Duke of Edinburgh, passes through the cheering crowds which packed Trafalgar Square to greet the Sovereign on her way to Buckingham Palace

A Souvenir
of the Coronation of
HER MAJESTY QUEEN ELIZABETH II
1953

Left: **1953** Prince Charles looking solemn as he stands, chin on hand, between The Queen Mother and Princess Margaret in the Royal Box at Westminster Abbey, from where he saw The Queen crowned. *Above left:* **1953** The front of the Coronation souvenir presentation holder. *Above:* **1953** A portrait of Queen Elizabeth II wearing the Imperial State Crown, taken in Buckingham Palace after her Coronation. *Right:* **1953** Queen Elizabeth II leads the procession following her Coronation ceremony in Westminster Abbey, London

Win a luxurious break for two on the Isles of Scilly

Lying just off the Cornish coast the Isles of Scilly are a haven of white sand beaches, azure seas, castles, tropical gardens and deserted paths all waiting to be explored and discovered by you. We are offering our readers the chance to win a three night break for two, inclusive of return Skybus flights from any of the 5 departure airports: Land's End , Newquay, Exter, Bristol or Southampton and staying at the luxurious St Mary's Hall Hotel on St Mary's.

St Mary's Hall Hotel is an elegant, extensively refurbished townhouse, where service and attention to detail are key. Their rooms are light, bright and fresh, with large beds, soft white towels and the little luxuries designed to make your stay comfortable and relaxing. With a restaurant, Spirit, using the finest produce for its seasonal menus and Revive, a treatment room, offering a variety of refreshing therapies this is the perfect base for you to make the most of these beautiful islands. www.stmaryshallhotel.co.uk, Tel 01720 422 316

Skybus is Cornwall's longest serving airline and affectionately known as 'the Islands' own airline.' The fleet of six light aircraft carry more than 60,000 people a year to the Isles of Scilly, and this year marks the 75th anniversary of fixed wing flights from Land's End to St Mary's.

To enter simply go to www.britain-magazine.com/ios-competition
Fill in your details and wait to hear from us.

St Mary's Hall Hotel
the Spirit of Scilly

www.stmaryshallhotel.co.uk

Skybus   Scillonian

Cruise from **Penzance** or Fly from **Land's End** • **Newquay** • **Exeter** • **Bristol** • **Southampton**
Call **0845 710 5555** or visit **www.ios-travel.co.uk**   IOSTravel   Isles of Scilly Travel   ATOL exe

Above: **1953** The spectacular view of the crowds lining The Mall, seen from the roof of Buckingham Palace as the Gold State Coach conveys The Queen and The Duke of Edinburgh to Westminster Abbey for the Coronation ceremony. Westminster Abbey has witnessed 38 coronations: the first to be documented was that of William the Conqueror in 1066.
Below: **1953** Queen Elizabeth II, Prince Charles, Princess Anne, The Duke of Edinburgh, The Queen Mother, and The Duke of Gloucester gather on the balcony of Buckingham Palace to view the fly past of the Royal Air Force following the Coronation. The young Prince and Princess take centre stage as they delight in the spectacle

LUCKNAM PARK
HOTEL & SPA, BATH

World Class Spa • Michelin Star Restaurant • Equestrian Centre
Tripadvisor Traveller's Choice Award 2012 • AA Hotel of the Year England 2010-11

A 1720 Palladian Mansion set in a 500 acre parkland just
6 miles from the historic City of Bath, a World Heritage Site

RELAIS &
CHATEAUX

Lucknam Park Hotel & Spa, Colerne, Chippenham, Wiltshire SN14 8AZ
Tel: +44 (0)1225 742777   reservations@lucknampark.co.uk   www.lucknampark.co.uk

Above: **1957** As The Queen and The Duke of Edinburgh pass the lovely Cobo Bay on the west coast of Guernsey, during their tour of the Channel Islands, both holidaymakers and local fishermen turned out in force to wish them well. The Duke of Edinburgh tipped his hat in recognition of the warmth and affection shown for the couple during their trip

Clockwise from above: **1953** Queen Elizabeth II laughs with The Duke of Gloucester as they watch the Olympic horse trials at Badminton, Gloucestershire; **1957** The Queen stops to chat to the American star Judy Garland following the Royal Variety Performance at the London Palladium; **1961** The Queen is well guarded atop an elephant on a tiger hunt in Nepal. The Queen and Prince Philip were guests of Nepal's King Mahendra on the hunt near Kathmandu; **1956** Queen Elizabeth II walks past a guard of yeoman warders from the Tower of London; **1952** The Queen making her first Christmas Day broadcast, at the Sandringham Estate, Norfolk

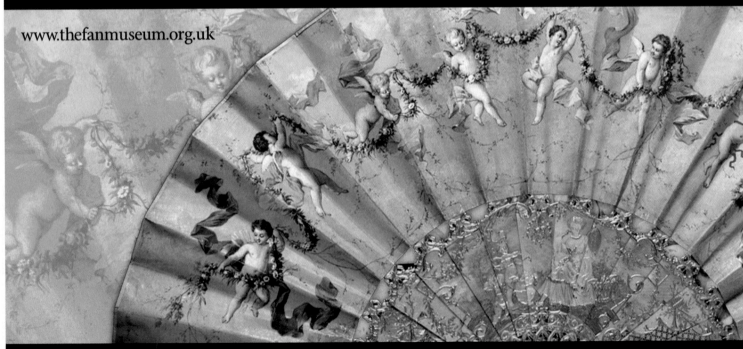

Above: **1957** With a little help from their father, The Prince of Wales and his sister Princess Anne play on a see-saw made from a log and a plank of wood. The siblings were watched closely by their parents. The family were visiting a sawmill on the Balmoral Estate during their holidays. *Below:* **1957** The Queen and The Duke of Edinburgh look up at the rigging of the Cutty Sark ship, which The Queen opened at its new permanent berth near the National Maritime Museum at Greenwich in London, that year. The Cutty Sark, which was once the fastest ship on the "China run", will undergo a major restoration project and reopen to the public during the Diamond Jubilee year

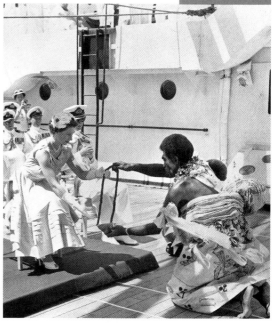

Opposite page: **1959** Royal Yacht Britannia with the Detroit skyline in the background during a tour of Canada. *Clockwise from above:* **1960** The Royal Family holidaying at Balmoral Castle, Scotland; **1953** The Queen receives gifts aboard the Royal Liner SS Gothic off Suva, Fiji; **1957** Formal dinner at the Waldorf-Astoria Hotel in New York; **1961** President John Kennedy and his wife pictured with The Queen and The Duke of Edinburgh at Buckingham Palace; **1956** The Queen shakes hands with Marilyn Monroe at the Royal Command Film Performance; **1959** The Queen smiles, on the last leg of the 45-day, 15,000-mile tour of Canada

Left: **1952** Queen Elizabeth II's first Trooping the Colour as monarch. Although The Queen was born on 21 April, it has long been the tradition to celebrate the Sovereign's birthday publicly on a day during the summer.
Above: **1953** On holiday at Balmoral, Scotland where The Queen, Prince Charles and Princess Anne relax on a garden bench with Her Majesty's corgi, Sue, standing guard in the background. *Below:* **1957** The Duke of Edinburgh, followed by The Queen with Prince Charles and Princess Anne both wearing kilts, on holiday at Balmoral. Purchased by Queen Victoria in 1848, Balmoral has been the Scottish home of the Royal Family ever since

FLORIS
LONDON

As sole Perfumers By Appointment to Her Majesty The Queen Elizabeth II
Floris are delighted to congratulate The Queen on Her Diamond Jubilee.

ROYAL ARMS
DIAMOND EDITION

In April 1926 a perfume was created at 89 Jermyn Street, London by the Floris family to celebrate the birth of King George V's first grandchild, Elizabeth. The fragrance was named 'Royal Arms'. On 2nd June 1953, Great Britain saw the Coronation of this grandchild as Her Majesty The Queen Elizabeth II took Her place at the throne.

Now, as sole Perfumers By Appointment to Her Majesty The Queen, this historic year of 2012 presents Floris with the opportunity to mark a momentous occasion.

To celebrate The Queen's Diamond Jubilee, Floris has brought to light the original 'Royal Arms' recipe and created an adaptation of this special perfume, which has then been hand poured into just six antique bottles.

The heart of this beautifully poised floral fragrance comes from the queen of flowers, the rose. Rose essence is balanced in a bouquet of jasmine, iris with ylang ylang and hints of sweet violet. Bergamot and lemon lift the heart of the perfume which is warmed by a nostalgic powdery base of amber, musk, patchouli and vanilla.

Perfume is the ultimate expression of a fragrance. Precious blended oils impart the most intimate character of the fragrance to the wearer.

The crystal bottle, dating back to the early 1900s is a classic and rare dressing table piece, each one of very few remaining in the Floris collection. The bottle is dressed simply with a 50 point fair trade white diamond, hand set by a London jeweller. Suspended on a delicate chain, the 18 carat solid gold decoration is finished with a hallmarked charm engraved 'Royal Arms'.

ESTABLISHED 1730
J. Floris Limited,
89 Jermyn Street, London SW1Y 6JH
www.florislondon.com

1962–1972
A Winning Combination

Although the Sixties were a time of great change for Britain, The Queen, who is known to enjoy life's simple pleasures, continues to combine her role as wife, mother and monarch with apparent ease and obvious devotion

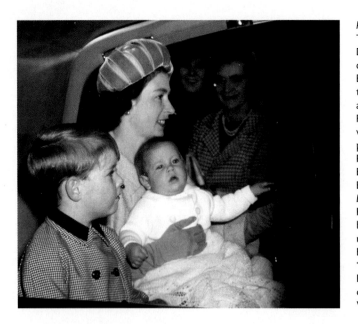

Previous page: **1972** The Queen and The Duke of Edinburgh during a visit to Balmoral to celebrate their Silver Wedding anniversary; **1966** FIFA World Cup final where The Queen presented the Jules Rimet trophy to England captain Bobby Moore. *Left:* **1964** With sons Prince Andrew and a baby Prince Edward returning from Balmoral. *Right:* **1968** The Royal Family in the grounds of Frogmore House, Windsor, Berkshire

A fter the globe-trotting first decade of her reign, The Queen's focus returned to family matters. Following the birth of her fourth child, Prince Edward in 1964, Buckingham Palace was keen to portray Her Majesty as a wife and mother who was in touch with the lives of her subjects. Photographs duly showed The Queen in motherly mode, devoid of any of the trappings of monarchy.

The Swinging Sixties marked a time of great change for Britain and The Queen embraced it. She handed out MBEs to the Beatles in 1965 and then a year later was front and centre of the biggest triumph in British football history when she presented England captain Bobby Moore with the World Cup trophy at Wembley.

The Commonwealth, however, was far from neglected with The Queen undertaking tours to Canada and the Caribbean and twice returning to Australia and New Zealand, in 1963 and 1970. It was during the latter trip Down Under that The Queen performed her first ever "walkabout", meeting ordinary members of the public.

Efforts to usher the monarchy into the modern era continued with the televising of Prince Charles's investiture at Caernarfon Castle on July 1, 1969. But the most ground-breaking footage of the royals came on Christmas Day that year when The Queen's traditional message was replaced with the television documentary "Royal Family". The brain-child of Prince Philip, the fly-on-the-wall exposé was intended to show the public that the Royal Family was not a "secret society" but just like everyone else. The world watched in wonder as the Duke of Edinburgh fried sausages at a Balmoral barbecue and The Queen was shown making small talk with guests, telling US President Richard Nixon: "World problems are so complex, aren't they now?"

WHERE THE MAGIC HAPPENS

The Lord's Tour is an ideal way to experience the magic of the world's most historic cricket ground.

Our knowledgeable and enthusiastic tour guides take you behind the scenes at the Home of Cricket, visiting the Honours Boards in the Players' Dressing Rooms, the Long Room, the J.P. Morgan Media Centre and the iconic Ashes Urn.

BOOK YOUR LORD'S TOUR NOW
www.lords.org/tours
020 7616 8595 | tours@lords.org

JOIN US ON A TOUR OF THE BBC

To book your tour of a BBC Building near you, please visit **bbc.co.uk/showsandtours** or call **0370 901 1227*** for group bookings.

facebook Join us on Facebook at facebook.com/bbctours

*UK wide rate charged at no more than 01/02 geographic numbers. Calls may be recorded for training.

Above: **1966** The Queen and The Duke of Edinburgh visit the disaster village of Aberfan, South Wales, to view flowers banked on a grave in the hillside cemetery of 82 of the 147 victims of the coal-tip avalanche.
Left: **1968** On a State Tour of South America, The Queen smiles after giving a cup to Pele, the world-famous soccer player, at a stadium in Rio de Janeiro, Brazil

Right: **1962** HM Queen Elizabeth II, The Queen Mother and Prince Andrew on board a train at King's Cross Station, London, as they leave for their Christmas holiday at Sandringham
Below: **1965** Onlookers admire the giant words on the Kinsley Wood plantation, Panpunton Hill, Radnorshire. The larch trees were planted by the Forestry Commission at the time of The Queen's Coronation in 1953

St Paul's.
An inside view

Inside St Paul's discover the tombs and memorials of some of the nation's greatest heroes.

There is so much to see and do at St Paul's Cathedral. The Crypt, The Monuments, The Art, The Whispering Gallery and one of the best views in London from the Golden Gallery. Use a touch screen multimedia guide, join a guided tour, or take part in an immersive film experience. Visit St Paul's and discover more than you would expect.

**Monday - Saturday 8.30am - 4pm
(except on special occasions)**
www.stpauls.co.uk

St PAUL'S
CATHEDRAL

HOUSES OF PARLIAMENT

SUMMER DATES ON SALE

OPEN SATURDAYS, YEAR ROUND

AWARD WINNING GUIDED TOURS

To book tickets please call +44 (0)844 847 1672, for groups call +44 (0)844 847 2498 or visit
www.ticketmaster.co.uk/housesofparliament
www.parliament.uk

The 2011 Group Travel Awards

ticketmaster

Above: **1972** The Royal Family sitting for a photographic portrait at Buckingham Palace, London. (Left to right) Prince Charles, Prince of Wales; Prince Edward; Queen Elizabeth II and her husband Prince Philip, Duke of Edinburgh; Prince Andrew, and The Princess Royal, Princess Anne, who is sporting the height of 70s fashion. *Below left:* **1965** The Queen laughs at a private joke with her trainer, Captain Boyd-Rochfort, before the Derby Stakes at Epsom Downs Racecourse, Surrey on 2 June. *Below right:* **1962** The two sisters looking very stylish – The Queen, Princess Margaret and the family corgis, arriving at London Airport having been aboard an RAF Comet jet from Scotland

Above: **1969** HM The Queen adjusts the robe of Prince Charles during his investiture as The Prince of Wales. The 20-year-old Prince received the Insignia as the 21st Prince of Wales at a ceremony within the medieval walls of Caernarfon Castle in front of 4,000 guests. Thousands more were in the dry moat and outside the castle, and millions around the world watched on television. The Queen invested The Prince with the Insignia of his Principality and Earldom of Chester: a sword, coronet, mantle, gold ring and gold rod

Clockwise from above: **1969** This photograph is one of a series taken at Windsor Castle to show the informal life of Prince Charles during the year of his investiture; **1963** Her Majesty The Queen, riding side-saddle, as she returns to Buckingham Palace, London, after attending the Trooping the Colour ceremony on Horse Guards Parade; **1965** The Queen is welcomed home by Mr Harold Wilson, the Prime Minister, when she arrives at Waterloo station, London, following her ten-day State Visit to Germany; **1965** Queen Elizabeth II and her youngest son, Prince Edward, aged 15 months, pictured in a sitting room at Windsor Castle, Berkshire

Left: **1965** The Queen and The Duke of Edinburgh lead mourners inside St Paul's Cathedral, London, during the funeral service for Sir Winston Churchill.
Below: **1970** Queen Elizabeth II, pictured with US President Richard Nixon, right, and Britain's Prime Minister Edward Heath at Chequers, Buckinghamshire

Left: **1969** Looking elegant, The Queen stands out from the crowd of "stuffy suits". HM The Queen is opening the new Victoria Underground line. Although she travelled on it as a child, this was the first time a reigning monarch had ridden on the London Underground

Spend a third of your life in first class

savoirbeds.co.uk

London 7 Wigmore Street, W1 555 Kings Road, SW6 Harrods, Knightsbridge, SW1 +44 (0)20 7493 4444

SAVOIR BEDS
SINCE 1905

London Paris New York Miami Berlin Stockholm Prague Beijing New Delhi

1972–1982

Silver Celebrations

The Queen encourages reconciliation and represents stability during years of economic insecurity in the UK and worldwide. Despite the difficulties, the country pauses to celebrate The Queen's Silver Jubilee

The celebrations to mark The Queen's Silver Jubilee in 1977 were a brief respite from the industrial disputes that had plagued Britain in the 1970s. Millions around the world took part in large-scale parties and parades to mark the 25th anniversary of The Queen's accession to the throne, culminating in June with the Jubilee Days to mark The Queen's official birthday following her turning 50 the year before.

Cementing her reputation as the most travelled monarch in royal history, The Queen undertook an unprecedented tour of Britain, visiting 36 counties with Prince Philip. A record one million-strong crowd turned out to see them in Lancashire. Their tour took them from the Pacific Islands of Western Samoa, Tonga and Fiji, through Australasia to Canada and the Caribbean.

It was a double cause for jubilation with The Queen and Prince Philip also celebrating their 30th wedding anniversary that year.

Indeed, it was one of Her Majesty's luckiest decades. In 1974 horse racing – "the Sport of Kings" – became the "Sport of Queens" when her own-bred filly Highclere galloped to victory in the 1,000 Guineas and the Prix de Diane. Champagne corks continued to pop for the birth of The Queen's first grandson, Princess Anne's son Peter Phillips, in 1977, and then again for The Queen Mother's 80th birthday in 1980.

But it was on July 29, 1981 when the festivities reached fever pitch for the marriage of Prince Charles to Lady Diana Spencer. Billed as a "fairytale wedding", it was watched by a global audience of 750 million while 600,000 people lined the streets to catch a glimpse of Diana en route to the ceremony at St Paul's Cathedral. Her ivory gown had an eight-metre train!

In 1982, The Queen hosted Ronald Reagan at Windsor Castle, once again flying the flag for Anglo-American relations.

Above: **1980** The Queen Mother blows out the candle on her cake during a special gala night in honour of her 80th birthday, at the Royal Opera House, London. *Far left:* **1977** Queen Elizabeth II on a walkabout among the crowds in Perth, Scotland, during her Silver Jubilee Tour of Britain. *Bottom left:* **1978** The Queen, together with her grandson, Peter Phillips, and his mother, Princess Anne, during the Christmas Day broadcast

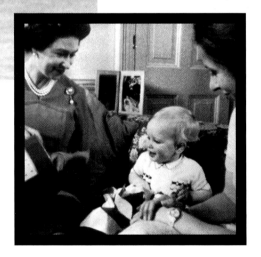

Left: **1977** The Gold State Coach at St Paul's Cathedral after bringing The Queen and The Duke of Edinburgh to attend a special service of thanksgiving for the Silver Jubilee. *Above:* **1982** Come rain or shine, The Queen's role is an all weather one. One of the daily hazards is the unpredictable British weather. After the Trooping the Colour ceremony, The Queen – riding on Burmese – canters back to Buckingham Palace, London, in the pouring rain, to appear on the balcony for the fly past by the RAF

Left: **1981** Prince Charles, Prince of Wales and Diana, Princess of Wales leave St Paul's Cathedral in London following their wedding on July 29, 1981, which was watched by millions globally. *Above:* **1982** Prince Charles and Princess Diana look on as The Queen rocks with mirth after shaking hands with the shot putter Geoff Capes at Braemar Highland Games. Capes had won the caber tossing and warned that he had not washed off the resin used to improve his grip, but Her Majesty still shook hands. *Below:* **1981** Prince Charles kisses his new bride, Lady Diana Spencer, the new Princess of Wales, on the balcony of Buckingham Palace in London. The Queen, on the right, chose a powder blue outfit for the day

Right: **1982** Queen Elizabeth II visiting the most famous street in Britain, when she and The Duke of Edinburgh toured the newly built outdoor location in Manchester for Granada Television's long-running programme Coronation Street. She is applauded by many of the long-serving and famous cast

Above: **1980** As part of her 80th birthday celebration, The Queen Mother visited the Press Club on Shoe Lane in London and tried her hand at snooker. *Right:* **1977** Queen Elizabeth II and The Duke of Edinburgh on the balcony at Buckingham Palace after the Silver Jubilee, joined by (from left) Prince Charles, Prince Edward, Princess Anne, Lord Mountbatten, Princess Margaret, Prince Andrew and The Queen Mother

Above: **1975** Standing on a stone bridge, Queen Elizabeth II views the garden of the Sento Gosho Palace in Kyoto, Japan. *Right:* **1975** The Queen proves she is a natural when it comes to tea drinking, as she sips green tea during a tea ceremony in the Garden of the Katsura Imperial Villa in Kyoto. She toured the ancient Japanese capital during her State Visit

Opposite page: **1977** The Queen and Prince Edward shield their ears at RAF Finningley, during the Silver Jubilee Review of the Royal Air Force. *Clockwise from above:* **1976** US President Ford and The Queen dancing during a State dinner. **1981** Corgi puppies being carried on to a plane at London's Heathrow Airport. **1977:** US President Jimmy Carter speaks with The Queen and The Queen Mother as Prince Philip and Italian Prime Minister Giulio Andreotti look on. **1973:** Royal concentration at Badminton Horse Trials. **1976:** The Queen laughs as a young girl was reluctant to hand over a bouquet of flowers during the Royal visit to Luxembourg

Above: **1982** The Queen with US President Ronald Reagan, at the start of an hour-long ride in Windsor Home Park. *Left:* **1976** The Queen stops for a word with Sir Charles Chaplin during the official opening of the International Centre of the British Academy of Film and Television Arts, in London. *Right:* **1977** Queen Elizabeth II turns photographer during a visit to the Lindsay Park Stud in South Australia

Discover the high life

Make your holiday one to remember by staying in a luxurious British retreat that's full of character, charm and style. Find the perfect place to stay...

Visit holidaylettings.co.uk/**inspire**me

from £275 per week

Home 177077

Home 14400

Cotswold cottages

For a quintessentially English break, stay in a cute thatched cottage nestled in the idyllic Cotswold countryside.

Home 183008

Perfect for large groups

Home 132262

English manor houses

Feel like lord and lady of the manor by spending your holiday at a grand manor house on a private estate.

Home 191738

Cheaper than a hotel

Live it up!

Home 142077

Apartments in London

Rent a stylish and spacious apartment for the Diamond Jubilee celebrations and save money per person.

Home 190719

from £542 per week

Home 190719

Castles in Scotland

Immerse yourself in the local history and legends of a medieval castle that was once the home of Scottish gentry.

holiday**lettings**™.co.uk
from ◎◎ tripadvisor®

1982–1992

Onwards & Upwards

During a decade of firsts, The Queen continued to lead the world's most famous Royal Family with a firm resolve, while Britain's then Prime Minister Margaret Thatcher ruled with an iron fist, and the media went weak at the knees over Princess Diana

Previous page left: **1986** An emotional moment for The Queen inside the fire damaged south wing of the 16th century Hampton Court Palace. *Previous page right*: **1983** The Royal Family gather on the balcony of Buckingham Palace to watch a fly past. *Opposite page*: **1986** The Queen and The Duke of Edinburgh on the Great Wall of China on the third day of their State Visit of China. *Right*: **1984** The Queen with her grandchildren Zara and Peter Phillips at Windsor Great Park. *Below*: **1989** The Queen holds a teddy bear she had received for her granddaughter Beatrice when she opened Royal Mint Court, Tower Bridge, London

The Falklands conflict of 1982 affected The Queen not only as Head of State but also as a mother when Prince Andrew was drafted into a Royal Navy task force sent to defend the islands following the Argentine invasion. When his aircraft carrier HMS *Invincible* returned to Portsmouth, The Queen and Prince Philip were among the families welcoming the vessel home.

The decade also had happier times; the birth of Prince William on June 21, 1982 proved a highlight for The Queen, who by the end of the decade was a proud grandmother of six.

In a decade of historical firsts, The Queen became the first monarch to visit China and then continued to help draw back the Iron Curtain by welcoming Russian president Mikhail Gorbachev to Windsor Castle, just six months before the fall of the Berlin Wall. She also paid a seminal State Visit to Iceland and undertook Commonwealth tours to no fewer than 20 countries including three visits to Australia and two to New Zealand.

Media interest in the royals intensified in the 1980s as Princess Diana continued to court the press and the public with her style icon status and controversial charitable causes. The Queen was not impervious to publicity, however, and there were reports that she was worried that the then Prime Minister Margaret Thatcher's economic policies would foster social divisions.

Newspapers reported that she was alarmed by high unemployment, rioting, the miners' strike and Thatcher's refusal to apply sanctions to the apartheid regime in South Africa. The Queen stuck to her trusted mantra: "Never complain, never explain." In fact the two most powerful women in Britain were fond of each other; when Thatcher left office in 1990, The Queen bestowed two honours on the Iron Lady as a personal gift.

MORE THAN AN ADDRESS, CHEVAL RESIDENCES ARE
YOUR KEY TO RELAXED CITY LIVING IN LONDON.
WITH 24-HOUR SECURITY, CONCIERGE AND HOUSEKEEPING
SERVICES ON SITE, WE LOOK AFTER THE DETAILS FOR YOU.

DETAILS THAT MAKE THE DIFFERENCE

Above: **1983** The Queen and Mother Teresa in New Delhi, India. The frail Roman Catholic nun won a Nobel award in 1979 for her work with the poor. *Below:* **1985** Prime Minister Margaret Thatcher is joined by The Queen and five former prime ministers at 10 Downing Street, London, as she hosts a dinner celebrating the 250th anniversary of the residence becoming the London home of prime ministers. *Left to right*: James Callaghan, Alec-Douglas-Home, Margaret Thatcher, Harold Macmillan, The Queen, Harold Wilson and Edward Heath

Above: **1982** The Prince and Princess of Wales introducing their son Prince William to the media for the first time. *Below left:* **1983** Queen Elizabeth II waves to some 300 residents of Grand Cayman from the deck of a sport fisherman boat, as she prepares to sail from Morgan Harbour to Cayman Kai. Seen with The Queen are Prince Philip on her right and Governor Lloyd of Grand Cayman on her left. *Right:* **1984** The Queen opening the £460-million Thames Barrier at Woolwich, London

ocklands

Opposite page: **1991** Peter Phillips, son of Princess Anne, escorts his grandmother through the grounds of his school. The Queen was at the school in Shaftesbury to open a new gymnastics hall. *Clockwise from above:* **1984** A young Prince William steals the limelight at the christening of his brother Prince Harry; **1991** The Queen and The Duchess of York with The Duke of York on board his ship, HMS Campbeltown, before it left harbour; **1989** The Queen and the Soviet leader Mikhail Gorbachev, during his visit to Windsor Castle; **1987** The Queen chats with the Lord Mayor of London, Sir David Rowe-Ham, in a computer-controlled Docklands Light Railway carriage in East London after she had opened the new transport system

Above: **1984** The Queen, when she delivered her Christmas Day message from the Oak Room of Windsor Castle, dressed in green jade and sitting by a desk with part of the castle shown through the window in the background; *Below:* **1990** Prince Harry celebrating his sixth birthday with his mother Princess Diana, The Duchess of York and The Duke and Duchess of Kent. Prince Harry points to the flyover of 168 military aircraft in honour of the 50th anniversary of the Battle of Britain. The fly past was the biggest ever since the Coronation

Left: **1991** The Queen Mother, followed by The Queen, meets well-wishers on her 91st birthday, outside Sandringham Parish Church; *Below left:* **1991** The Queen smiles as her sister Princess Margaret moves away a Christmas decoration during a visit to the backstage facilities at London's Royal Opera House. Earlier they had watched a rehearsal of the Royal Ballet's Christmas show, The Nutcracker; *Below right:* **1988** The Queen and The Queen Mother watch Derby Day at Epsom

Explore England's treasures with Old English Inns

The Red Lion, Adderbury

The Woolpack, Beckington

Rothley Court, Rothley

The Lamb, Ely

From just £99

for two people for two nights, including breakfast

If you've something to celebrate, or feel you're in need of a well-deserved break, give yourself a treat in the heart of the English countryside – and save pounds into the bargain.

We have over 50 suggestions of where you can take your spring, summer, autumn or winter break in an Old English Inn – many steeped in history and all oozing tradition. And you'll find the buildings are every bit as fascinating as their settings.

You'll fall in love with the cosy bars, often with crooked walls and low beams, where you can relax and enjoy some delicious food and real cask ales.

Perfect for touring, walking, visiting historic houses and gardens or just putting your feet up in a comfy armchair.

To take advantage of this offer **BOOK ONLINE** at **www.oldenglishinns.co.uk** call **0845 60 86 072** or email **central.reservations@oldenglish.co.uk** quoting **JUBILEE.**

OldEnglish INNS

NEWQUAY holiday lettings

www.newquayholidaylettings.co.uk
enquiries@newquayholidaylettings.co.uk

1992–2002

Trying Times

During difficult times, most families seek comfort behind closed doors and in quiet moments. But when The Royal Family faced a decade marred by personal tragedy and public scrutiny – all eyes were upon them

orever remembered as Her Majesty's "annus horribilis", 1992 was not a good year for the House of Windsor. In a speech delivered at Guildhall to mark the 40th anniversary of her accession, The Queen admitted: "1992 is not a year on which I shall look back with undiluted pleasure." Just four days before, a fire had ripped through her favourite royal residence – Windsor Castle – destroying some of the most historic parts of the building. Three out of four of The Queen's children also announced their marriage separations that year. In the same speech she said: "I sometimes wonder how future generations will judge the events of this tumultuous year."

There was some welcome cheer in 1994 when The Queen opened the Channel Tunnel, travelling on the Eurostar with Prince Philip for the very first time.

The Royal Family was out in force to mark the 50th anniversary of VE-Day in 1995, joining the hundreds of thousands who gathered to pay tribute to those who fought for peace. The commemorations culminated in a spectacular fly past over Buckingham Palace. Nelson Mandela's State Visit the following year once again brought the crowds out in The Mall. There was a huge greeting for the South African president, who, the year before, had hosted The Queen and Prince Philip on their tour of the newly liberated nation.

There was to be yet more tragedy for the Royal Family. The Queen was in Balmoral with Princes Charles, William and Harry when they learned of the death of Princess Diana on August 31, 1997. Criticised for being out of touch with her grieving subjects, The Queen gave the most poignant public address of her reign when she paid tribute to Diana, speaking not only as Queen but "as a grandmother."

The new millennium was a double cause for celebration with the Queen Mother turning 100 and receiving a telegram from her daughter. But the decade ended as badly as it started. Within days of The Queen marking the 50th anniversary of her accession, her sister Princess Margaret passed away, followed by The Queen Mother just six weeks later.

Previous page: **1999** Queen Elizabeth II inspects the First Battalion and Number Seven Company of the Coldstream Guards. Her Majesty presented new Colours to the regiments at Windsor Castle in her capacity as Colonel-in-Chief. *Above left:* **1998** The Queen attends the ceremonial service for the Order of the Bath at Westminster Abbey. The name derives from the medieval ceremony for creating a knight, which involved bathing as one of its elements. *Above:* **1998** The annual Garter ceremony at Windsor Castle, Berkshire

Above: **1995** The Queen shakes Sir Cliff Richard's hand following his appearance at the Royal Variety performance at the Dominion Theatre in London. Richard was knighted earlier the same year. Standing next to him are the singers Elaine Paige and Des O'Connor. *Below:* **1993** The Queen Mother and The Queen with Prince Michael of Kent admiring the new Queen Elizabeth gate, in Hyde Park, London. Prince Michael of Kent conceived the idea of constructing the £1.5 million gate as a tribute to his aunt, The Queen Mother, on her 90th birthday. Lord Rogers, the architect, described the design by the sculptor David Wynne as "romantic candyfloss" and compared the design to one of Queen Elizabeth's hats

Above: **1994** The Queen and The Duke of Edinburgh travelling on the new Eurostar train. Her Majesty opened Waterloo International Station, before the couple boarded the Eurostar to Calais Coquelles for the inauguration of the Channel Tunnel with President Mitterrand of France. The Eurostar now departs from St Pancras. *Below:* **2000** The Queen Mother, with her two daughters Princess Margaret and The Queen, and the Duke of Edinburgh. The Queen Mother waves to the crowds from the balcony of Buckingham Palace to celebrate her 100th birthday. Earlier, The Queen Mother received a birthday card from her daughter The Queen, who signed the personal greeting "Lilibet" – her childhood name

Left: **1997** The Queen Mother and The Queen at the funeral of Diana, Princess of Wales at Westminster Abbey, London. *Below:* **1997** The Queen and The Duke of Edinburgh view the many floral tributes to Diana at Buckingham Palace. Diana's death was met with extraordinary public expressions of grief, and her funeral on 6 September, 1997 drew an estimated three million mourners and onlookers in London, as well as worldwide television coverage. The Royal Family's initial decision not to return to London or to mourn more publicly was much criticised at the time, and their rigid adherence to protocol was interpreted by some as a lack of compassion

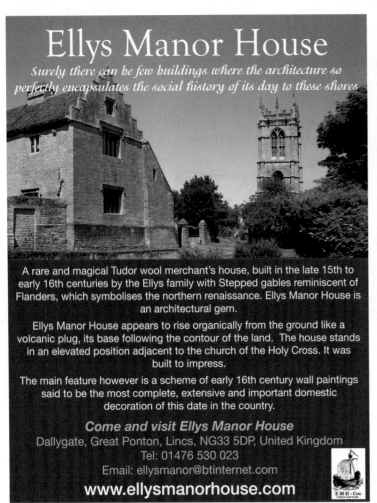
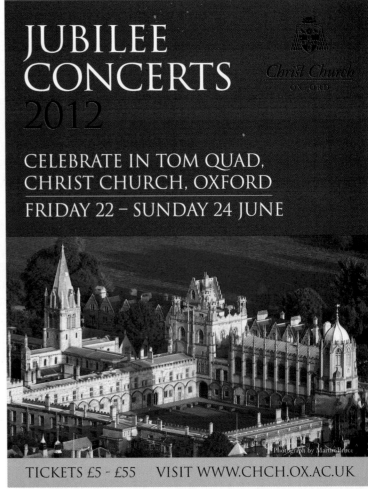
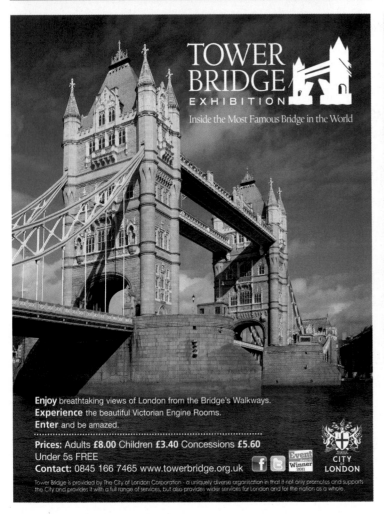
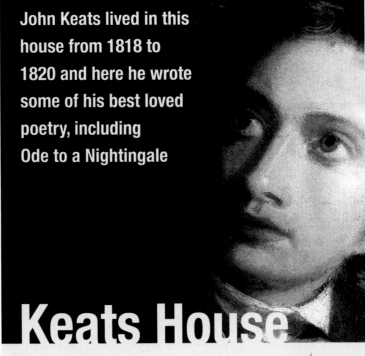

Above left: **1992** Firemen tackle the blaze that ripped through Windsor Castle and threatened one of the greatest collections of art in the world, while an aerial view shows Windsor Castle still smouldering after the fire. *Above right:* **1992** The Queen surveys the damage caused by the fire. *Right:* **2002** The Queen watches as the coffin containing the body of The Queen Mother is put into a hearse following the funeral service. In the background, Princes William and Edward bow their heads in respect, as a tearful Prince Charles salutes

Above: **1998** The Queen encountered an old acquaintance during a visit to the Roman site of Vindolanda near Hadrian's Wall in Northumberland; a corgi bred by The Queen and now owned by Lady Beaumont who lives in the area. *Below:* **1996** Nelson Mandela, President of South Africa, and The Queen ride in a carriage along The Mall on the first full day of his State Visit to Britain. It was an historic moment as it was the first State Visit by a South African president. Prince Charles and Nelson Mandela later went on a "walkabout" in Brixton, south London, where they were greeted by thousands of people, before addressing tens of thousands in Trafalgar Square from the balcony of South Africa House

2002–2012

The Diamond Queen

Her Majesty Queen Elizabeth II and the country celebrated first a Golden Jubilee, then a wonderful wedding where The Duke and Duchess of Cambridge captured everyone's heart. Now we witness only the second monarch ever to celebrate a Diamond Jubilee – sixty splendid years as Sovereign!

Previous page: **2002** The Queen rides in the Gold State Coach from Buckingham Palace to St Paul's Cathedral for a service of thanksgiving to celebrate her Golden Jubilee. Along the way she shares the special moment, waving to enthusiastic crowds. *Below left:* **2011** William and Kate's eight-tiered wedding cake made by Fiona Cairns. *Right:* **2011** Prince William and his bride Catherine – now The Duke and Duchess of Cambridge – arrive at Buckingham Palace for their reception after their wonderful wedding at Westminster Abbey, London

T he decade began with The Queen still grieving over the deaths of her beloved mother and sister within two months of each other, she had no choice but to look forward to the Golden Jubilee in 2002. The glittering celebrations extended beyond the Commonwealth, with even the pinnacle of the Empire State Building in New York lit in royal purple and gold in The Queen's honour. In Britain the commemorations, which culminated with rock group Queen's Brian May strumming *God Save the Queen* from the roof of Buckingham Palace, reaffirmed the popularity of the Royal Family after the turbulent 1990s.

Despite approaching her 80th birthday, The Queen covered more than 40,000 miles with Prince Philip, visiting the Caribbean, Australia, New Zealand and touring the UK before wrapping up the Jubilee year in Canada.

April 9, 2005 proved to be a seminal date for the Royal Family when Prince Charles married Camilla Parker Bowles at the Windsor Guildhall. Although The Queen did not attend the civil wedding ceremony, she was present at the blessing and later gave a humourous speech about the bride and groom at the reception.

Yet the event was to be upstaged by the biggest Royal Wedding of them all when Prince William married Catherine Middleton on April 29, 2011. A staggering two billion people were said to have tuned into the ceremony from around the world.

Within weeks it was business as usual at Buckingham Palace when The Queen welcomed President Obama and his wife on a State Visit. 2011 also saw another extraordinary historic first in The Queen visiting the Republic of Ireland, the first monarch to do so since George V almost 100 years earlier. It was the perfect prelude to yet another landmark in The Queen's reign. Her Majesty's 60 years on the throne, marked with wonderful events including a Pageant on the River Thames, a concert at Buckingham Palace and a service of thanksgiving at St Paul's Cathedral.

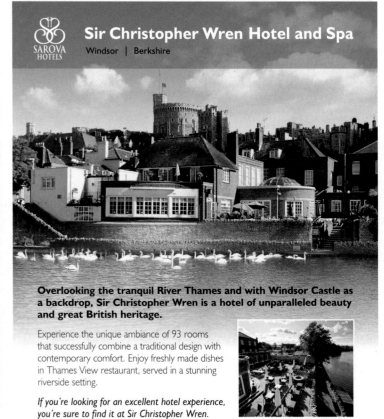

Clockwise from right: **2011** The Queen chats to Carole Middleton, the bride's mother, as The Duchess of Cornwall and other members of the Royal Family emerge from Westminster Abbey after the wedding ceremony of Prince William and Kate Middleton; **2011** View of the Victoria Memorial and The Mall filled with thousands of well-wishers celebrating the Royal Wedding during the flyover; **2011** Catherine, Duchess of Cambridge and Prince William looking radiant and relaxed as they leave Westminster Abbey following their marriage ceremony

Above: **2011** Lady Louise Windsor, the elder child and only daughter of Prince Edward, Earl of Wessex and Sophie, Countess of Wessex with Prince Harry – who was Prince William's "best man", rather than "supporter", as is royal tradition – wave to the crowds during the procession to Buckingham Palace after the wedding ceremony at Westminster Abbey.
Below: **2011** Prince William and Kate Middleton with her father Michael Middleton at Westminster Abbey, London, just moments before the wedding ceremony begins. Prince William and Catherine wrote their own prayer for the service. It began: "God our Father, we thank you for our families; for the love that we share and for the joy of our marriage"

Above: **2011** British "bobbies" ahead of a sea of red, white and blue on The Mall in London as thousands of people head towards Buckingham Palace to watch Prince William and his new bride on the balcony. The "kiss" is the hotly awaited moment, and the couple did not disappoint their adoring crowd. *Below:* **2011** Prince William and his bride, now The Duchess of Cambridge, followed by best man Prince Harry and maid of honour Pippa Middleton – Catherine's younger sister – leaving Westminster Abbey in London following the wedding service. The Duchess's dress was designed by Sarah Burton for Alexander McQueen, with close input from Her Royal Highness

Above: **2011** Prince William and his new bride walk down the aisle at Westminster Abbey, London, following their marriage. Prince William wears the uniform of Colonel of the Irish Guards – he is commissioned in all three Armed Services and this is the uniform of his senior honorary appointment in the Army. *Right:* **2011** Following their wedding ceremony, the newly married Duke and Duchess of Cambridge are conveyed along the Procession Route to Buckingham Palace in a 1902 State Landau

Above: **2006** Queen Elizabeth II sits in the Regency Room at Buckingham Palace in London as she looks at some of the cards which have been sent to her for her 80th birthday. Buckingham Palace revealed she had received 20,000 cards and 17,000 e-mails and the delighted Queen said: "I would like to thank the many thousands of people from this country and overseas who have sent me cards and messages on my 80th birthday." *Below:* **2011** The Queen signs the guest book as she bids farewell to US President Barack Obama and First Lady Michelle Obama, watched by The Duke of Edinburgh at Winfield House – the residence of the Ambassador of the United States of America – in Regent's Park, London

Above: **2005** The Prince of Wales and his new bride Camilla, Duchess of Cornwall with their families (back row, left to right) Prince Harry, Prince William, Tom and Laura Parker Bowles, (front row, left to right) The Duke of Edinburgh, HM Queen Elizabeth II and Camilla's father Major Bruce Shand. The picture was taken in the White Drawing Room at Windsor Castle, following a civil ceremony at Windsor Guildhall and a Church of England service of blessing at St George's Chapel

Clockwise from above: **2010** The Queen is presented with a Tube station sign during a visit to Aldgate, London; **2009** Warmly elegant at the unveiling of a statue of The Queen Mother in The Mall, London; **2008** Tossing a puck ahead of a friendly ice-hockey match in Slovakia – on the first-ever visit to the country; **2009** Signing the visitors' book, during a visit to Lisneal College, in Londonderry, at the start of a three-day tour of Northern Ireland; **2002** David Beckham and Kirsty Howard hand the Jubilee Baton to The Queen after its final leg around Manchester

2007 HM Queen Elizabeth II and her husband HRH The Duke of Edinburgh are joined at Clarence House by members of their family on the occasion of a dinner hosted by HRH The Prince of Wales and HRH The Duchess of Cornwall to mark the Diamond Wedding Anniversary of The Queen and The Duke

Above: **2006** Britain's Prince Harry, second from the right, grins and his grandmother Queen Elizabeth II smiles, as she inspects the Sovereign's Parade at the Royal Military Academy in Sandhurst, England. The parade takes place at the end of each term to mark the passing out of Officer Cadets who have completed the Commissioning Course. *Left:* **2011** Prince William shows The Queen the hangar where the Sea King Helicopter he flew during his training as a Search and Rescue pilot is kept, during a visit to RAF Valley in Anglesey, Wales. *Below:* **2006** The Queen inspects the graduates, including a smiling Prince William, in the Sovereign's Parade at Sandhurst

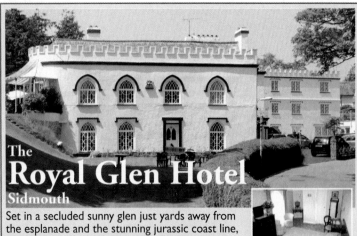
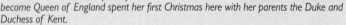

Clockwise from above: **2005** Leaving St Mary and St George (Anglican) Church following a service in Jasper, Canada; **2008** Unveiling a familiar looking bronze statue at Baden-Powell House, London; **2011** Speaking at Dublin Castle during a State Dinner on the second day of Her Majesty's State Visit to Ireland; **2007** Admiring One's wedding gown – on show at the Summer Opening Exhibition at Buckingham Palace, to mark The Queen's Diamond Wedding Anniversary; **2006** The Queen and The Prince of Wales, joking at the Braemar Highland Games

PHOTO: PRESS ASSOCIATION /TIMGRAHAM

Above: **2007** To mark their Diamond Wedding Anniversary on November 20, 2007 Queen Elizabeth II and Prince Philip, The Duke of Edinburgh re-visit Broadlands where, 60 years ago in 1947, they spent their wedding night. Broadlands in Hampshire had been the home of Prince Philip's uncle, Earl Mountbatten. *Below:* **2008** The Queen views the painting of the Queen Elizabeth II liner, which she unveiled during her final visit to the ship at Southampton docks. The liner – often referred to as QE2 – was built for Cunard and operated by them as a liner and cruise ship from 1969 to 2008. Following her retirement from cruising, the QE2 was acquired by an investment company in Dubai

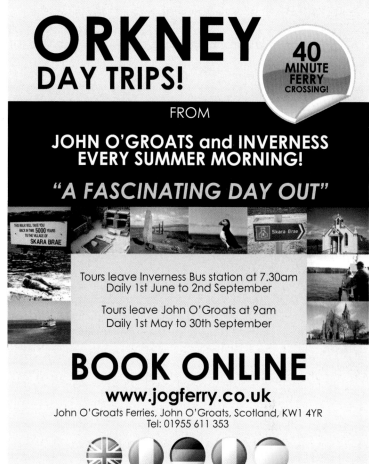

The Royal Residences

The chequered history, the memorable occasions, the sumptuous interiors and the imposing architecture of Britain's royal residences make these buildings some of the nation's greatest treasures. From the relatively recent splendour of Buckingham Palace, to forgotten gems such as Kew Palace and the Castle of Mey – these are the country's grandest homes

View from St James's Park towards the Victoria Memorial outside Buckingham Palace, which serves as The Queen's home for most of the year

PHOTO: © LOOP IMAGES/PAWEL LIBERA

Main image: Buckingham Palace. *Below right:* The Palace's Blue Drawing Room. *Below left:* Royal Grenadier Guard on attention outside the Palace wearing a traditional bearskin hat

O f all Britain's iconic images, that of Buckingham Palace is probably conjured up the most. Yet it isn't quite as ageless as it might seem: that familiar view – the magisterial 104m-long (340ft) eastern front, stern yet dignified along The Mall – isn't even 100 years old. In terms of royal residences, it is very much the youthful upstart.

Buckingham House, as it was originally known, had an entirely un-royal beginning. Dating from 1705, it was built as a country retreat (the adjacent St James's Park adding a relative degree of rurality to this part of London) for the Duke of Buckingham. At something like 28m x 14m (90ft x 45ft), it was far more modest than the building we see today. Only in 1762 did its royal pedigree commence when it became the home of Queen Charlotte, wife of George III. The building then underwent a prolonged period of growth – the following 18 years seeing various additions by the architect Sir William Chambers.

▶

Windsor Castle is the largest and oldest occupied castle in the world, encapsulating 900 years of British history and covering an area of 26 acres

George IV had every intention of making Buckingham Palace his principal residence, commissioning John Nash – his much-favoured architect – to improve it. Arguably, Nash's greatest "palatial" legacy is the fact that he went hugely over budget; materially, he did at least give us the western façade overlooking the palace gardens.

William IV, George's brother, had no liking for the place at all – optimistically offering it as a replacement for the Houses of Parliament when they burned down in 1834. Only in 1837, when Queen Victoria moved in, did it become a fully functioning royal residence – a role it has maintained ever since. Even then, there was still work to be done, resulting in additions by Edward Blore, Thomas Cubitt and Sir Aston Webb – the latter refaced the eastern front in 1913.

It is that fully functioning role that makes today's palace unique. While serving as The Queen's home for most of the year, it is still very much a "place of business" – hosting state and ceremonial banquets, prime ministerial and diplomatic audiences, and investitures.

Buckingham Palace, however, is not the only royal residence to have humble beginnings. Queen Victoria and Prince Albert found Balmoral Castle, the Scottish home of the Royal Family, far too small when they purchased it in 1852. Within months, Albert had commissioned William Smith (Aberdeen's city architect) to build a new one and by 1856 Balmoral was complete. With its fairytale turrets, this most enchanting of royal homes is little changed today – a diamond set amid an extensive estate, and still much enjoyed by the Royal Family.

Similarly, when The Prince of Wales, later to be Edward VII, acquired the Sandringham Estate in 1862, it did not take too long for him to conclude that its house (then in a bad state of repair) was nowhere near large enough. He had it demolished, the main body of the new house being ready by 1870. It is, however, just a small part of a 20,000-acre estate. Both George V and George VI were especially fond of this Norfolk retreat, and it is still used regularly by the Royal Family – notably during the Christmas season.

If Buckingham Palace is the youthful interloper, then in terms of royal residences, Windsor Castle sits ▶

robustly at the head of the family tree. Built by William the Conqueror as a wooden structure on the site of a Saxon fort (where the Round Tower, the principal feature of today's castle, stands), it has evolved to become the largest occupied castle in the world.

By the 12th century, Henry II had used stone to make it more substantial and during the 14th century Edward III undertook the rebuilding and expansion. He also founded, in 1348, the Most Noble Order of the Garter, Britain's highest-ranking form of chivalry. Its patron saint is St George and its place of worship is the castle's St George's Chapel, which took over 50 years to build and was completed in 1528. Several kings are buried here, among them Henry VI, Edward IV, Henry VIII, a beheaded Charles I, and George VI.

But it was George IV who was responsible for much of the castle as we see it today. His father, George III, had already instigated a metamorphosis from castle to palace and, upon ascending the throne, his son continued the work. His principal architect was Jeffry Wyatt, whose uncle James Wyatt had formerly worked on the castle for George III.

Jeffry's work included adding to and improving the State Apartments. The Waterloo Chamber, a banqueting hall commemorating Napoleon's defeat, is generally considered his finest work. Among the rewards for his efforts (and for spending over £300,000 in the process), Wyatt received a knighthood – and the change of his name to Wyatville.

Unbowed by the turbulence and truculences of 900 years of history, it was only in the late 20th century that Windsor Castle almost fell. On November 20, 1992, fire broke out in the private apartments. Among the rooms subsequently gutted were St George's Hall (until the building of the Waterloo Chamber, the main banqueting hall) and the Grand Reception Room. Good fortune meant that most of the treasures had previously been removed to facilitate restoration work and losses were minimal. A huge repair programme started almost immediately, the result being that visitors today hardly know that anything happened.

With the progression of time, some royal homes have fallen out of favour. Some, such as Greenwich Palace, are long disappeared. Others, from The Queen ▶

Previous pages (left to right): **The Garter Throne Room in Windsor Castle; Windsor Castle's King's Bedchamber.** *Above:* **View of the Georgian section of Hampton Court Palace, and the formal gardens.** *Below:* **Heraldic animals adorn the imposing entrance.** *Opposite page:* **Kew Palace became a Royal Palace in 1781**

Mother's Castle of Mey on Scotland's northern tip, to Victoria and Albert's deeply loved Osborne House on the Isle of Wight, remain.

Kew Palace is a fine example of a residence disused by royalty. This red brick Jacobean mansion, variously known as the Dutch House (after the Flemish merchant who built it in 1631) and the Old Palace, is the sole survivor of several royal buildings that have stood on the site. At 65ft x 47ft, it is certainly small, but was nevertheless especially liked by George III. It was also a convenient and relatively isolated place for the King to be dispatched to during his spells of mental instability – although ill health meant his final visit was to be 14 years before his death. His Queen, Charlotte, died here in 1818.

From then on, the palace was never again used as a long-term royal residence. It was Queen Victoria who first opened it to the public, and it underwent a multi-million pound restoration during the 1990s.

Hampton Court Palace has suffered a similar falling from grace, last being used as a royal residence by George II. Cardinal Wolsey built it in 1521, with the intention of creating the most impressive home in Britain. And he clearly wanted to show it off – there were almost 300 guest bedrooms.

Wolsey, however, fell out of favour with his volatile king (Henry VIII), and, in an attempt to salvage the situation, gifted him the palace. This appears to have done little for Wolsey's prospects, even if the king seemed mightily pleased by his acquisition. Henry moved in almost at once and subsequently it was to be home to five of his six wives.

Other royal residents included Edward VI, Elizabeth I – who ensured that the interior was increasingly sumptuously appointed – and Charles II. William and Mary then engaged Christopher Wren to undertake improvements and so interested were they in proceedings that they virtually assumed the mantle of clerk of the works. Initially, they briefed the famous architect to pull the entire place down in the name of modernisation (a plan curtailed by shortage of funds and Mary's early demise).

Later, George I, the German monarch, willingly retired to Hampton Court to escape a way of life with which he never quite seemed able to get to grips.

The hand of Wren is still readily evident – as is much of the original Tudor building, arguably Britain's finest. But again 20th-century disaster almost overtook previous events when fire broke out in the King's Apartments in March 1986. Once more, tragedy was averted and most of the interior's treasures were saved. Nonetheless, the extensive damage sustained took almost six years to rectify.

Returning north to Scotland, Edinburgh's Palace of Holyroodhouse is one of royalty's lesser known residences. The official home of The Queen in Scotland, it basks in the glow of being the only royal residence to be built next to a volcano – albeit a long-extinct one – Arthur's Seat.

King David I had built an abbey here during the 12th century; it served royal requirements for more than 300 years until an adjacent palace was built by James IV ▶

Clockwise from main:
Kensington Palace;
Queen Victoria spent her
childhood at the Palace,
having been born there
in 1819; Queen Mary's
Bedchamber

in 1498. It fell to Charles II and his architect William Bruce to commence the construction of the baroque building that we can see today. In its various guises, Holyrood has witnessed the Coronation of Charles I; served as home to Mary, Queen of Scots; and was a regular port of call for Queen Victoria.

Back in central London, Wren's work may again be seen in the form of Kensington Palace. The original house that stood on the site was acquired by William III in 1689: Wren was soon put to work to make the dwelling fit for a king and his queen.

Subsequently, it was much favoured by Queen Anne (she died here in 1714); even George I found time to enjoy the place – although apparently not the work of the still-toiling Wren, whom he dismissed. It then became the main home of George II (who also died here), after which it was used by members of the extended Royal Family.

Hence, it was to witness the birth and upbringing of Queen Victoria; in turn, one of her daughters lived here. More recently, it has been the home of Princess Margaret, and Prince Charles and Princess Diana

– the latter continued to reside here until her death in 1997. It is now the official London residence of The Duke and Duchess of Cambridge.

Two miles to the east of Kensington Palace, Clarence House was famously the home of Queen Elizabeth the Queen Mother. However, its royal pedigree extends beyond the 20th century. Another dwelling designed by John Nash (in 1828), it was built for the soon-to-be William IV – The Duke of Clarence. As King, he spent much of his time here.

Over the years, the splendid stucco building has been extended and the interior adapted to suit its residents' tastes. However, since William IV, no member of the Royal Family has lived here as monarch: rather, Clarence House is another building that has served as the private residence of various members of the extended Royal Family.

Thus, among others, it has been home to Queen Victoria's mother, Princess Margaret, and the ascendant and newly married Princess Elizabeth and Duke of Edinburgh. These days, in combination with the adjacent St James's Palace, it is the official ▶

Main: The Palace of Holyroodhouse. *Below:* The King's Bedchamber in Holyroodhouse contains the finest painting and carving in the Palace

London home of The Prince of Wales, The Duchess of Cornwall, and Prince Harry.

A passageway connects Clarence House with St James's Palace. Pre-dating its neighbour by almost 300 years, it was built in 1532 for Henry VIII. Especially known for its enchanting octagonal gateway towers, it has been subject to various additions and improvements over the years – not least when fire struck in 1809.

St James's became the Sovereign's official residence after the destruction of Whitehall Palace by fire in 1698. Accordingly, it is yet another building that has witnessed the trials and tribulations of royal and state life, and seen the births of both Charles II and James II.

Today, St James's continues to play a considerable role in affairs of state. It is where the Garter King of Arms announces the accession of a new sovereign and, curiously, is still considered the principal palace of the monarch – although none has lived here since William IV. Finally, diplomats traditionally present their credentials to the Court of St James's, although it actually happens at Buckingham Palace where this brief tour of some of Britain's royal residences began.

⌂ For more information about the Royal Palaces, Residences and Art Collection (which include the State Rooms, the Royal Mews and The Queen's Gallery at Buckingham Palace, Clarence House, Windsor Castle, Frogmore House and Palace of Holyroodhouse), visit *www.royalcollection.org.uk* or call +44 (0)20 7766 7300. For more information about the Historic Royal Palaces (which include Kensington Palace, Hampton Court Palace, Banqueting House, Kew Palace and Tower of London), visit *www.hrp.org.uk* or call +44 (0)20 3166 6000. To view images of all the residences mentioned in this feature, visit the BRITAIN website *www.britain-magazine.com*

Britain and the Diamond Jubilee Year

With dramatic pomp and ceremony in the capital, landmark exhibitions and events across the country, and sociable street parties in tucked-away villages, the long weekend of the Diamond Jubilee, and 2012 as a whole, will be one to remember. We round up some highlights to look forward to, and to look back on and remember this momentous year

One of the first actions to mark the Jubilee year was the announcement that Greenwich has been awarded Royal Borough status

A sense of anticipation is building around the country, plans are being finalised and preparations made for the plethora of exciting events and festivities organised for HM The Queen's Diamond Jubilee weekend and throughout the year. One of the first actions to mark the occasion, at the beginning of February, was the announcement that Greenwich has been awarded Royal Borough status – the first borough to be granted royal status in over 80 years.

Greenwich has been a royal manor since the early 15th century and the borough has significant associations with individual British monarchs and other members of the Royal Family, including Henry VIII who was born at Greenwich Palace in 1491. He married his first and fourth queens at the Palace (Catherine of Aragon and Anne of Cleves) and his son Edward VI also died there.

To confirm the borough's official royal status, a Royal Charter signed by The Queen was delivered to the Town Hall in Woolwich from the Office of the Lord Chancellor on February 3 and a weekend of celebrations took place following the announcement, including a magnificent fireworks finale next to the Old Royal Naval College.

Councillor Chris Roberts, Leader of Greenwich Council, said: "This is a proud day for Greenwich and its people, and reflects centuries of close associations between the Borough and the monarchy. It is a great honour for the Borough to receive the Royal Seal during Her Majesty's Diamond Jubilee year, and heralds the start of a truly unique year in the Borough's history."

The announcement also means that Greenwich will be the only Royal Borough among the six host boroughs for the London 2012 Games. Known globally as the home of the Prime Meridian, Greenwich Mean Time and a UNESCO World Heritage Site, this double honour will boost the borough's profile and provide a unique experience for spectators, visitors and residents alike.

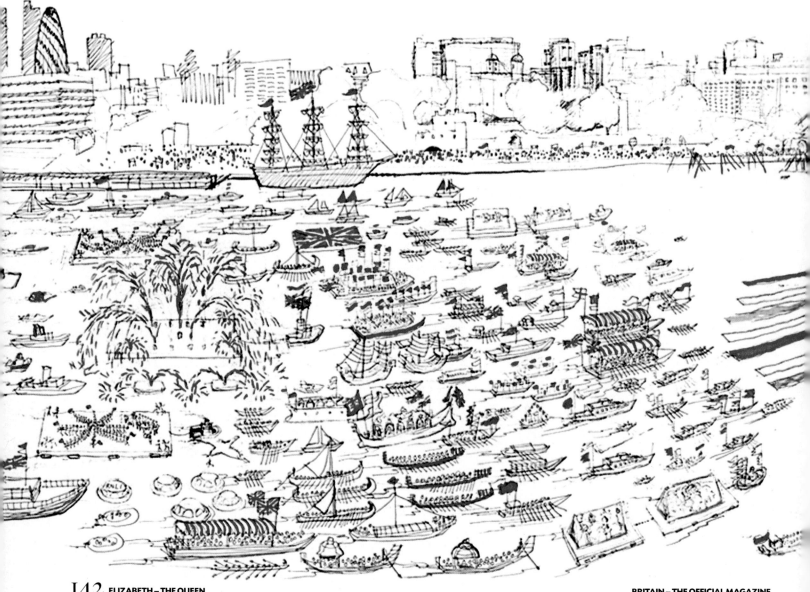

Dazzling displays

The central weekend to celebrate The Queen's Diamond Jubilee takes place from June 2-5, with an extra Bank Holiday so that the whole country can enjoy the festivities. The main event in London is the Thames Diamond Jubilee Pageant where more than 1,000 boats, assembled from across the UK, the Commonwealth and around the world will muster on the river. The flotilla will be one of the largest ever on the Thames and The Queen and The Duke of Edinburgh will travel in a Royal Barge as a centrepiece. During the weekend, The Queen will also attend the Epsom Derby on June 2, the BBC Concert at Buckingham Palace on June 4 and a Service of Thanksgiving at St Paul's Cathedral followed by a formal carriage procession.

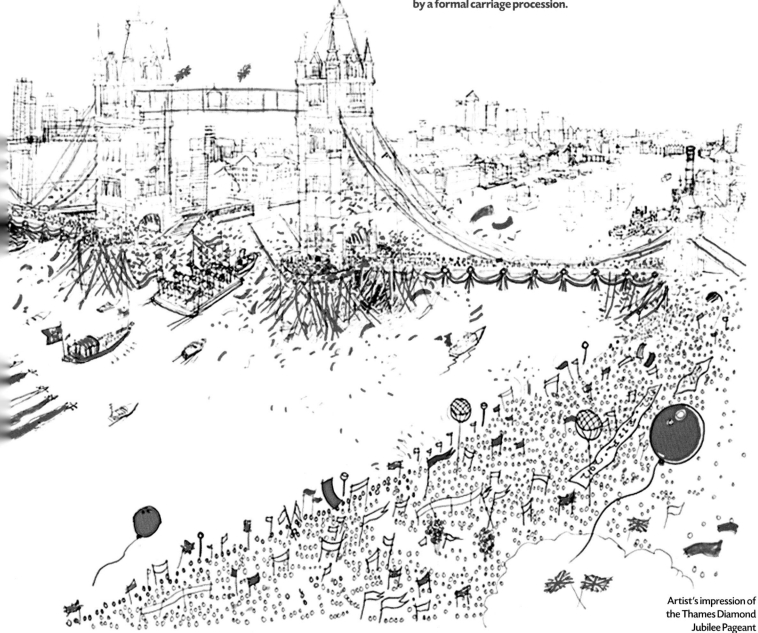

Artist's impression of the Thames Diamond Jubilee Pageant

Winning design

You'll have seen it on our front cover and on all kinds of Diamond Jubilee merchandise and promotional material – this official emblem is the winning design from 10-year-old Katherine Dewar, from Chester. Katherine won a national competition for children aged between 6 and 14, and her design symbolises the fun and celebratory feel of the event.

CECIL BEATON

Featuring portraits of The Queen by royal photographer Sir Cecil Beaton, including this one (*right*) taken at Buckingham Palace in March 1945, a new exhibition celebrates Her Majesty in her roles as princess, monarch and mother. The photographs of the British Royal Family by Beaton were central to shaping the monarchy's public image in the mid-20th century and The Queen was still a young princess when she first sat for Beaton in 1942. Over the next three decades he was invited to photograph her on many significant occasions, including her Coronation Day in 1953. "Queen Elizabeth II by Cecil Beaton" runs until April 22 at London's Victoria & Albert Museum before touring Britain and the Commonwealth.

CROWN JEWELS
Dress up for the occasion in this Tatty Devine tiara, £126.

WWW.TATTYDEVINE.COM

NATIONWIDE

PHOTOS: V&A IMAGES/TATTY DEVINE/ARTHUR EDWARDS, MBE © THE SUN

CELEBRATIONS IN ROYAL WINDSOR

The Queen's childhood home and weekend retreat at Windsor Castle is celebrating her Jubilee in style. A new exhibition called **"The Queen: 60 Photographs for 60 Years"** has opened to the public, featuring images of Her Majesty from leading press photographers of the past six decades. The exhibition presents a portrait of her reign as captured in fleeting moments on official occasions and at relaxed family gatherings.

Windsor is also holding a **Diamond Jubilee Pageant** that

will take place in the private grounds of Windsor Castle on the evenings of May 10-13.

Dancers, musicians, military and equestrian displays from around the world will come together for three nights in a performance to pay tribute to 60 spectacular years of The Queen's reign.

And the 2012 **Royal Windsor Horse Show** will feature some of the

acts from the Diamond Jubilee Pageant as well as over 3,000 horses and ponies, including Her Majesty's own, taking part in more than 170 classes from May 9-13.

FIESTA FESTIVAL

Eastbourne's Jubilee celebrations – the Fiesta – run from June 2-4. A Sunshine Carnival signals the start of the festival, bringing together a dazzling array of costumes, dressed floats and dancers in a seafront procession, ending in a spectacular party. Eastbourne Cultural Communities Network follows on Sunday with a day of global fusion, featuring food, music and dance. And the Monday will celebrate The Queen's 60th year with a live music stage, classic motor cavalcade and a dressed flotilla of yachts.

EASTBOURNE

NATIONWIDE

The Big Jubilee Lunch

The Big Jubilee Lunch on June 3 will build on the already popular Big Lunch initiative, and people will be encouraged to share lunch with neighbours and friends as part of the Diamond Jubilee celebrations. This could take the form of a traditional street party, a picnic lunch, or any other get-together that fosters a simple act of community, friendship and fun. Some 10 million people came out in 1977 to celebrate the Silver Jubilee and it is hoped many more will in 2012.

JUBILEE TOURS

Capital Sport has a number of new cycling and walking tours, including one in celebration of the Diamond Jubilee staying in historic four-star hotels.

WWW.CAPITAL-SPORT.CO.UK

THAMES

NATIONWIDE

LIGHT THE BEACONS

2,012 Diamond Jubilee Beacons will be lit across the UK, Channel Islands, Isle of Man, the Commonwealth and other countries as part of the celebrations to mark the Jubilee. This image shows the VE-Day Beacon at Ross-on-Wye's famous Prospect.

Bounteous Biscuiteers

The Biscuiteers love a bit of British pomp and ceremony and have created some of the prettiest Jubilee-themed treats we've seen. And better still – they taste delicious too. Mark Her Majesty's Jubilee with a tin of beautifully hand-iced biscuits featuring corgis, crowns and gilded coaches; a royal collection of chocolates; or even a chubby little Union Jack cake. You'll be the envy of your Big Lunch neighbours!

BRITAIN'S CATHEDRALS

The Diamond Jubilee exhibition at Southwell Minster will run from May 19 until June 17. The Minster will be showing 26 paintings from the Royal Collection as well as a set of 17th-century paintings from Ripon Cathedral. A black-tie gala dinner will mark the opening night private view on May 18.

Gloucester Cathedral will be holding Pomp & Circumstance – Concert for The Queen on June 2 featuring the Gloucester Choral Society and the music of Parry, Handel, Walton and Elgar, which was performed at The Queen's Coronation in 1953.

Guildford Cathedral is holding a "Diamond Dinner" on Friday May 11. The evening of dinner, jazz, a cabaret act, art, and a live auction in the

nave of Guildford Cathedral will raise much needed funds to keep this wonderful building in good condition for future generations.

THE QUEEN'S JEWELS

During the summer opening of Buckingham Palace in August and September a spectacular exhibition will show the many ways in which diamonds have been used by British monarchs over the last 200 years. "Diamonds: A Jubilee Celebration" includes an unprecedented display of a number of The Queen's personal jewels – those inherited by Her Majesty or acquired during her reign. The exhibition will reveal how many of these stones have undergone transformations during their history.

LONDON

DEVON

Celebrate in Clovelly

The picturesque fishing village of Clovelly is uniquely special in that it has no cars and no individually owned houses. Its cottages tumble down a cleft in the 120-m (400ft) cliff along cobbled streets to a tiny working port and quay. A fabulous street party on June 2 in this most picturesque of streets will feature plenty of prizes to be won in a treasure hunt, for the best fancy dress and for the best portrait of The Queen, along with fun and games for the adults too.

PARK PAGEANT
On June 3 Battersea Park will play a key role in the public celebration of The Thames Diamond Jubilee Pageant.

LONDON

LONDON

LINKS TO ROYAL-TEA

The InterContinental London Park Lane has strong links to royalty, as The Queen was born on the site. To mark its unique heritage, The Wellington Lounge will be introducing its "Royal-Tea" from May, to celebrate the Jubilee. Tel: +44 (0)20 7409 3131.

Patriotic pottery

Deck out your home in red, white and blue with Emma Bridgewater's unashamedly celebratory Diamond Jubilee collection. The great British brand, which proudly makes all of its ware in the UK, has launched its biggest ever royal commemorative range, full of gorgeous pieces from Diamond Jubilee crockery to aprons, teatowels and more.

ROYAL TREASURES

"Treasures from The Queen's Palaces" in The Queen's Gallery at the Palace of Holyroodhouse runs from March 16 – September 16 and features some of the finest treasures from the Royal Collection. The exhibition reflects the tastes of monarchs who have shaped one of the world's great art collections. The selection of 100 outstanding works has been made across the entire breadth of the Royal Collection from eight royal residences and most of the works will be shown in Scotland for the first time.

EDINBURGH

SALISBURY

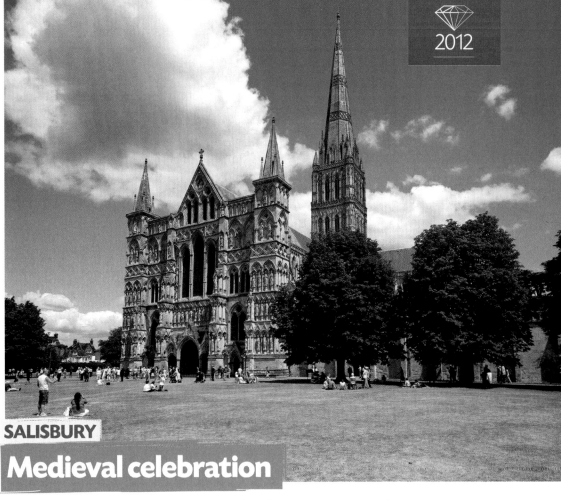

Medieval celebration

A host of one-off activities are planned in Salisbury to mark this once in a lifetime year of the Queen's Diamond Jubilee. In the beautiful Cathedral and surrounding Close on May 1, Wiltshire Council is planning a large medieval celebration event for all the family, with jousting tents, medieval-themed music and entertainment and a military display. On June 1 the Cathedral will also hold the "Wiltshire Celebration Service".

JUBILEE TOUR
The Mandarin Oriental Hyde Park is offering a unique four-day Diamond Jubilee Tour on June 2.
WWW.MANDARINORIENTAL.COM

LONDON

LINCOLNSHIRE

LANDSCAPE OF BRITAIN

Easton Walled Garden's "Summer Meadows" event on June 3-4 will celebrate England's summer meadows and coincides with the Jubilee weekend. It aims to educate visitors on the importance of protecting our natural landscape.

THE PERFECT PARTY

The beautiful country house and gardens of Polesden Lacey is one of the 2,012 sites chosen to light a beacon for the Jubilee. It will also be holding a "Right Royal Greville Day" on June 3-4 with Edwardian entertainment to celebrate the Jubilee in Royal style. Edwardian hostess Mrs Greville was the owner of Polesden Lacey from 1906 until her death in 1942 and was a friend of the royals. Visitors can lose themselves on the estate with its many walks and stunning views across the Surrey Hills, or feel like one of Mrs Greville's party guests and marvel at the house's lavishly decorated rooms.

SURREY

2012

BANGOR

Royal days out

With an extra long weekend for the Diamond Jubilee, June is the perfect time to visit some of Britain's National Trust properties, which offer lots of fantastic family days out with a royal theme. Among the delights and curiosities to be found at Penrhyn Castle, for example, is the one-ton slate bed specially made for the visit of Queen Victoria and Prince Albert in 1859 – Her Majesty refused to sleep in it after claiming it would have been like sleeping in a tomb!

THAMES PAGEANTRY

View Canaletto's Greenwich masterpiece at the National Maritime Museum's "Royal River" exhibition.

GREENWICH

FLYING THE FLAG

In this commemorative year luxury brand Linley is celebrating all things British with a striking collection of Union Flag accessories including these photo frames.

TEL: (020) 7730 7300 ; WWW.DAVIDLINLEY.COM

STAR OF THE SHOW

Cumbria is celebrating The Queen's Diamond Jubilee in style with Katherine Jenkins as she opens the Whitehaven Diamond Jubilee Festival. The singer will be joined by a host of other stars during the three days, which also feature tall ships, air displays, celebrity chefs, food stalls and lots of family activities, including a fun fair. Then the Royal Jubilee Festival of Fools on June 3-7 at Muncaster Castle offers five days of foolish Jubilee frivolity including a concert with the firing of Muncaster's Jubilee Cannons.

CUMBRIA

RICHMOND
Tea and culture

The Petersham Hotel in Richmond has created a special Diamond Jubilee Afternoon Tea, which is running in support of the Museum of Richmond's "Happy and Glorious" exhibition. The tea is available until June 23 and The Petersham will donate £1 from each tea sold to the museum. As well as hosting the exhibition, which looks at how local people have celebrated royal events over the last 150 years, the Royal Borough welcomes The Queen on May 15.

GLORIOUS YEARS

Join the Bowes Museum for a 50s outdoor event on June 3, with live music and a vintage clothes market.

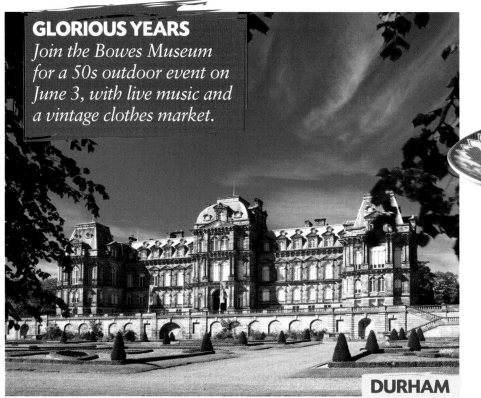

DURHAM

JUBILEE CHINA

Pieces from the official range of Diamond Jubilee commemorative china are sure to become collectors' items. It's available now from the Royal Collection shops.

WWW.ROYALCOLLECTION.ORG.UK/SHOP

TREAT YOURSELF

Grosvenor House has a long-standing royal connection, making it the perfect location to share in the Jubilee celebrations. Staying at London's most exclusive address on Park Lane, guests can feel like royalty themselves with the Jubilee package – an overnight stay in a luxurious Park View Suite, a sumptuous breakfast the following morning and a pair of tickets to the V&A's "Queen Elizabeth II by Cecil Beaton: A Diamond Jubilee Celebration" exhibition.
www.londongrosvenorhouse.co.uk

LONDON

NATIONWIDE

Sweet souvenir

We love this portrait of The Queen made entirely of Jelly Belly jelly beans that is doing the rounds of independent sweet stores, farm shops and garden centres in honour of the Jubilee. It took over 10,000 jelly beans and five weeks to create! The Queen has sat for 139 official portraits during her lifetime, two of which were with The Duke of Edinburgh. Her Majesty was just seven years old when she sat for her first portrait in 1933.

DELIGHTFUL GIFTS

Fortnum & Mason's beautiful Jubilee gifts have each been specially commissioned and decorated with a design inspired by The Queen's Beasts.

WWW.FORTNUMANDMASON.COM

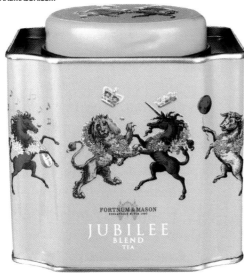

PICTURE THIS

"The Queen: Art & Image" exhibition brings together over 60 of the most remarkable and resonant portraits of The Queen.

NATIONWIDE

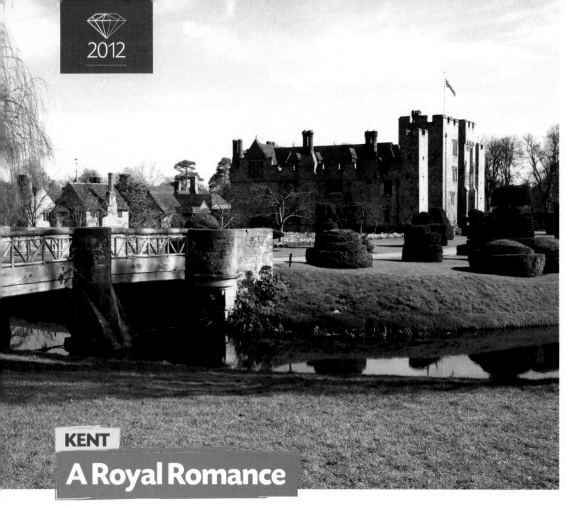

HAREWOOD HOUSE

Harewood House commemorates this special Jubilee year with two exhibitions – "Royal Harewood: Celebrating the Life of The Yorkshire Princess", and "Marcus Adams: Royal Photographer, photographs from the Royal Collection". Visitors will have a unique insight into the life of HRH Princess Mary in Yorkshire, including previously unseen items from her Faberge and Fan collection, many given as gifts when Harewood was a Royal Household. In the Terrace Gallery, intimate photographs of a young monarch to-be will be on view for the first time in the UK.

WEST YORKSHIRE

PHOTOS: © THE ROYAL COLLECTION/HEVER CASTLE & GARDENS

KENT

A Royal Romance

As the country celebrates the Diamond Jubilee, Hever Castle revisits the Coronation celebrations of one of its most famous occupants, Anne Boleyn, with a new exhibition in the Long Gallery. A Royal Romance includes a replica of Anne's Coronation gown and the colourful period is brought to life with an informative soundtrack of "court whispers" which tell of the intrigue and gossip that surrounded Anne's tempestuous relationship with Henry VIII.

JUBILEE WOODS

The Woodland Trust is helping people across the UK to plant six million trees in celebration of the Diamond Jubilee.

NATIONWIDE

COMMUNITY SPIRIT

This set of original colour postcards by the well-known British photographer Martin Parr takes an affectionate and humorous look at the Jubilee theme and the very British tradition of neighbourhood street parties.

WWW.ANOVABOOKS.COM

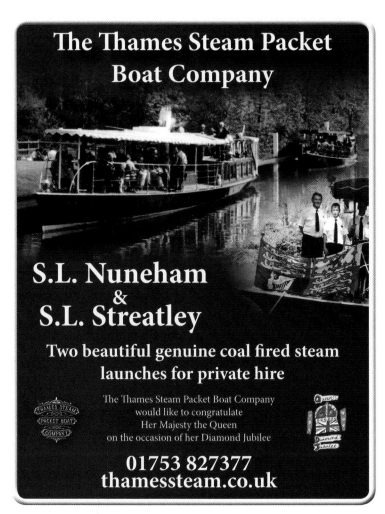
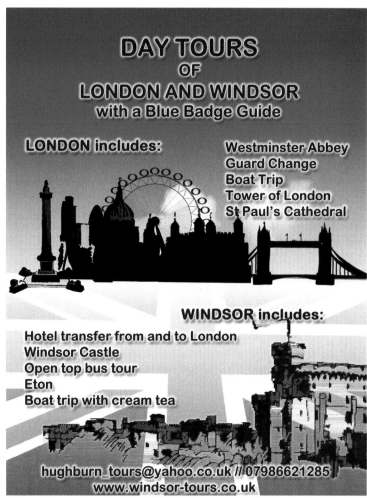

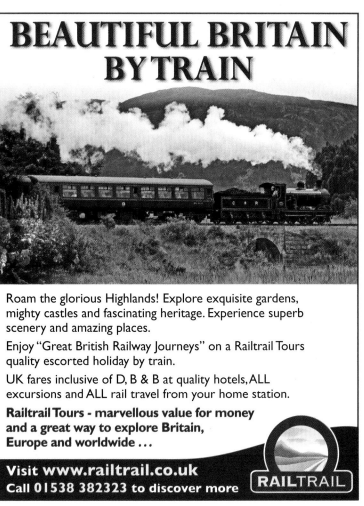

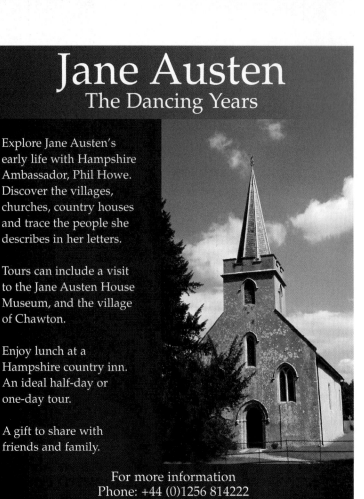

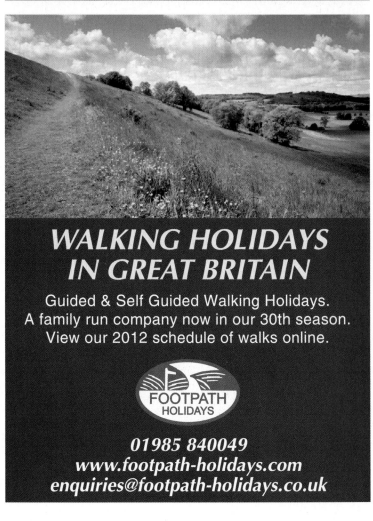

Left: A London family watches The Queen during her first Christmas day telecast (1957). *Below left:* Princess Elizabeth learns to tie knots at Buckingham Palace (1943)

60 facts for 60 years

Like many little girls, the young Princess Elizabeth acted in plays and became a Girl Guide, but not every child goes on to meet 12 prime ministers, three popes, the first man in space, or become Queen... We share some interesting facts about the life of Her Majesty Queen Elizabeth II

1 The Queen is the **40th monarch** since William the Conqueror became King of England.

2 She was the first British monarch since the Act of Union in 1801 to be out of the country at the moment of accession.

3 The Queen was **born on April 21, 1926**, but her official birthday is celebrated in June.

4 She was christened on May 29, 1926 at Buckingham Palace.

5 As a young girl, Princess Elizabeth **acted in a number of pantomimes** at Windsor Castle during World War Two and played the part of Prince Florizel in *Cinderella*.

6 She was a **Girl Guide** (1937) and a Sea Ranger (1943).

7 There have been six Archbishops of Canterbury during The Queen's reign – Geoffrey Fisher, Michael Ramsey, Donald Coggan, Robert Runcie, George Carey and Rowan Williams.

8 There have been six Roman Catholic popes during her reign (Pius XII, John XXIII, Paul VI, John Paul I, John Paul II, Benedict XVI).

9 The Queen has received two popes on visits to the UK (Pope John Paul II in 1982 and Pope Benedict XVI in 2010). Pope John Paul II's visit was the first papal visit to the United Kingdom for over 450 years. **The Queen has officially visited the Vatican twice** in her reign – she was there in 1961 visiting Pope John XXIII and in 1980 visiting Pope John Paul II.

10 The Queen is 5'4" (64 inches or 160cm) tall.

11 The Queen has been at the saluting base of her troops in every Trooping the Colour ceremony since the start of her reign, with the exception of

12 The Queen has broadcast a Christmas message every year since her coronation in 1952, except in 1969.

1955, when a national rail strike forced the parade's cancellation.

13 Every year The Queen sends Christmas trees to Westminster Abbey; Wellington Barracks; St Paul's Cathedral; St Giles and The Canongate Kirk, Edinburgh; Crathie Church; and local Sandringham schools and churches.

14 The Queen has an **extensive collection of jewellery**, most of which are Crown Jewels, some inherited and some gifts – including the largest pink diamond in the world.

15 The Royal Collection, a huge hoard of art including 150,000 paintings by masters such as Rubens, Rembrandt, Titian and Raphael, is held in trust by The Queen for the nation.

16 The Queen is the **first British monarch to have celebrated a Diamond Wedding Anniversary**.

17 **Princess Elizabeth and Prince Philip first met** when they attended the wedding of ▶

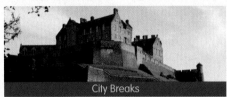

Prince Philip's cousin, Princess Marina of Greece, to The Duke of Kent in 1934.

18 The engagement between Princess Elizabeth and Lieutenant Philip Mountbatten was announced on July 9, 1947. Prince Philip was born Prince Philip of Greece and Denmark. He joined the Royal Navy in 1939 and after the war, in February 1947, became a naturalised British subject.

19 The Queen's platinum and diamond engagement ring was made by jewellers Philip Antrobus Ltd, using diamonds from a tiara belonging to Prince Philip's mother.

20 The Queen and The Duke of Edinburgh were **married in Westminister Abbey** on November 20, 1947 with 2,000 invited guests.

21 The Queen's **wedding dress was designed by Norman Hartnell** and was woven at Winterthur Silks Limited, Dunfermline, in the Canmore factory, using silk that had come from Chinese silkworms at Lullingstone Castle.

22 The Grave of the Unknown Warrior was the only stone that wasn't covered by a special carpet in the Abbey. The day after the wedding, Princess

Top right: Princess Elizabeth, left, and Princess Margaret in Cinderella (1942). *Above:* The Queen's corgis

Elizabeth followed a royal tradition, started by her mother, of sending her wedding bouquet back to the Abbey to be laid on this grave.

23 The Queen and Prince Philip received over **2,500 wedding presents** from well-wishers around the world. Most were put on display for a few days in a charity exhibition at St James's Palace. Other gifts, from members of the public, included a hand-knitted cardigan and tea cosy, and two pairs of bed socks.

24 Although he was The Queen's husband, **The Duke of Edinburgh was not crowned or anointed at the Coronation** ceremony in 1953. He was the first subject to pay homage to Her Majesty, by stating "I, Philip, Duke of Edinburgh, do become your liege man of life and limb, and of earthly worship; and faith and truth I will bear unto you, to live and die, against all manner of folks. So help me God."

25 Prince Philip has accompanied The Queen on all her Commonwealth tours and State Visits, as well as on public engagements in all parts of the UK. The first of these was the **Coronation Tour of the Commonwealth** from November 1953 to May 1954, when the couple visited Bermuda, Jamaica, Panama, Fiji, Tonga, New Zealand, Australia, Cocos Islands, Ceylon, Aden, Uganda, Libya, Malta and Gibraltar, travelling a massive distance of 43,618 miles.

26 In 60 years, The Queen has visited Australia 18 times, Canada 22 times, Jamaica six times and New Zealand 10 times.

27 The Queen has undertaken **261 official overseas visits**, including 78 State Visits, to 116 different countries.

28 The Queen speaks fluent French and often uses the language for audiences and State Visits.

29 With the birth of Prince Andrew in 1960, The Queen became the first reigning sovereign to have a child since Queen Victoria, who had her youngest child, Princess Beatrice, in 1857.

30 As well as corgis, The Queen breeds and trains Labradors and cocker spaniels at Sandringham.

31 The Queen's **first horse** was a Shetland pony given to her at age four by her grandfather, King George V. The little pony's name was Peggy.

32 Other strange animal gifts Her Majesty has received over the years, placed care of London Zoo, have included jaguars, sloths and racing pigeons.

33 The Queen sent **her first email** in 1976 from an army base.

34 The Queen takes a keen interest in horses and racing. She has about 25 horses in training each season. She also **continues to ride** at Sandringham, Balmoral and Windsor.

35 The Queen's **racing colours** are purple with gold braid, scarlet sleeves and black velvet cap with gold fringe. They were adopted from those used by King Edward VII; one of his most successful horses was called Diamond Jubilee.

➤

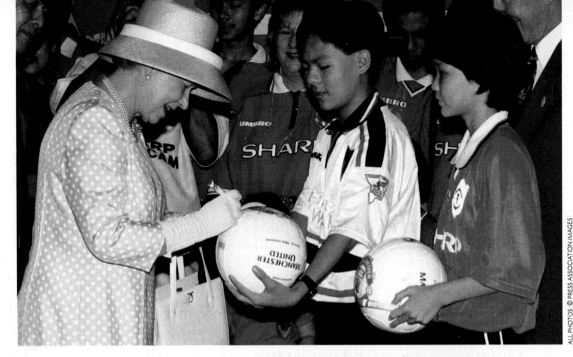

Right: The Queen signs a Manchester United football in Kuala Lumpur.
Below: Princess Elizabeth and her sister releasing a carrier pigeon in 1943

ALL PHOTOS: © PRESS ASSOCIATION IMAGES

36 All 5,300 breeding pairs of mute swan in Britain and all sturgeon, whales, porpoises and **dolphins in British waters are officially owned by The Queen**.

37 The Queen **learnt to drive in 1945**.

38 Princess Elizabeth **travelled on the London Underground for the first time in May 1939** with her governess Marion Crawford and Princess Margaret.

39 The Queen is patron of more than **600 charities** and organisations.

40 Her Majesty has attended **36 Royal Variety Performances**.

41 The Queen has sat for **129 portraits** during her reign, painted in a variety of styles.

42 The Queen has answered around three and a half million items of correspondence and sent more than **175,000 telegrams** to centenarians in the UK and the Commonwealth.

43 Since 1952 The Queen has given Royal Assent to more than 3,500 Acts of Parliament.

44 During the past 60 years, almost one and a half million people have attended garden parties at Buckingham Palace or the Palace of Holyroodhouse.

45 The Queen's reign has seen **12 different prime ministers** – from Sir Winston Churchill through to David Cameron.

46 Tony Blair is the first prime minister to have been born during her reign, in May 1953 – a month before the Coronation.

47 The Queen has gifted approximately **90,000 Christmas puddings** to staff, continuing the custom of King George V and King George VI.

48 The Queen has **30 godchildren**.

49 The Royal Yacht *Britannia* was first used by The Queen when Her Majesty embarked with The Duke of Edinburgh on May 1, 1954 at Tobruk for the final stage of their Commonwealth Tour. The last time The Queen was on board for an official visit was on August 9, 1997 to Arran in Scotland.

50 The Queen made an **historic visit to the Republic of Ireland** in May 2011, the first visit by a British monarch since Irish independence (King George V visited in 1911).

51 The Queen has **opened 15 bridges** in the UK.

52 The Queen has attended 56 Royal Maundy services in 43 Cathedrals during her reign. A total of 6,710 people have received Maundy Money in recognition of their service to the Church and their communities.

53 The first football match The Queen attended was the 1953 FA Cup Final.

54 The Queen **launched the British Monarchy's official website** in 1997. In 2007 the official British Monarchy YouTube channel was unveiled, followed by a Royal Twitter account (2009), Flickr site (2010) and Facebook page.

55 The Queen has owned more than **30 corgis** during her reign, starting with Susan who was a present for her 18th birthday in 1944. Her Majesty currently has three corgis – Monty, Willow and Holly.

56 The Queen also introduced a new breed of dog known as the "dorgi" when one of her corgis was mated with a dachshund.

57 The Queen hosted the first women-only event, Women of Achievement, at Buckingham Palace in March 2004.

58 The Queen has met the first astronauts to go into space, the first woman in space and the first man on the moon, at Buckingham Palace.

59 During the Silver Jubilee year, The Queen toured 36 counties in the UK and Northern Ireland, starting in Glasgow on May 17, 1977. During her Golden Jubilee year The Queen toured 35 counties, beginning in Cornwall on May 1, 2002.

60 Queen Victoria was the last and, to date, the only British monarch to celebrate a Diamond Jubilee. The Queen, who will be aged 85 on Accession Day in 2012, will be the oldest monarch to celebrate a Diamond Jubilee. Queen Victoria was 77 when she celebrated hers in 1897. ■